PENGUIN BOOKS

The Penguin Book
of Brexit Cartoons

The Penguin Book of Brexit Cartoons

PENGUIN BOOKS

PENGUIN BOOKS

UK | USA | Canada | Ireland | Australia
India | New Zealand | South Africa

Penguin Books is part of the Penguin Random House
group of companies whose addresses can be found at
global.penguinrandomhouse.com.

First published in 2018

012

Copyright © Penguin Books, 2018
The permissions on pp. 103–7 constitute
an extension of this copyright page

Typeset by Jouve (UK), Milton Keynes
Printed and bound in Great Britain by Clays Ltd, Elcograf S.p.A.

A CIP catalogue record for this book
is available from the British Library

ISBN: 978–0–141–99008–8

www.greenpenguin.co.uk

Penguin Random House is committed to a
sustainable future for our business, our readers
and our planet. This book is made from Forest
Stewardship Council® certified paper.

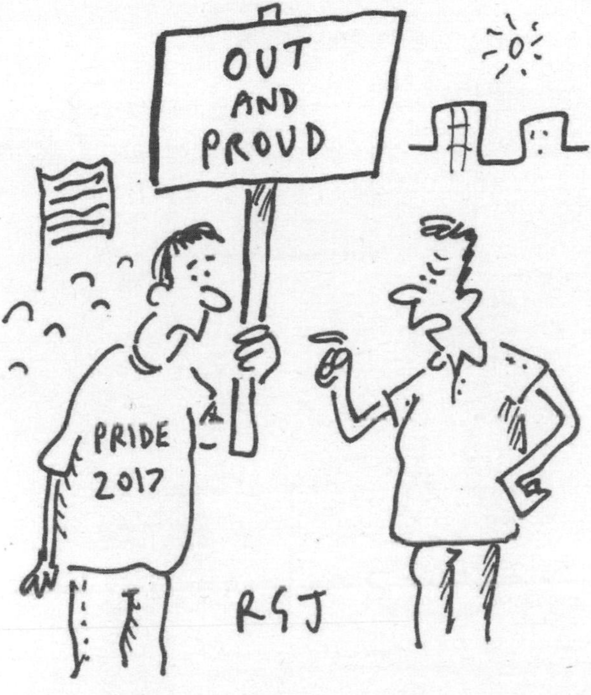
OUT
AND
PROUD
PRIDE
2017
RGJ

"BLOODY GLOATING BREXITERS"

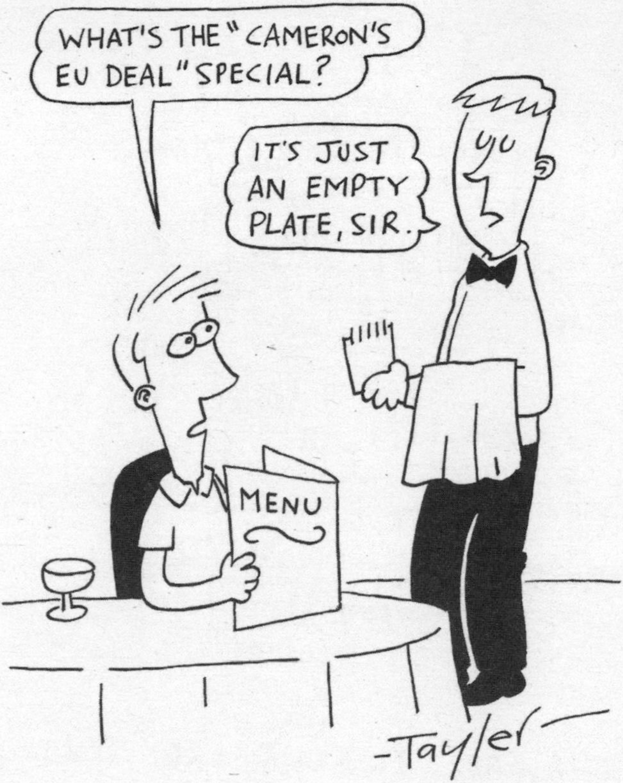
WHAT'S THE "CAMERON'S EU DEAL" SPECIAL?
IT'S JUST AN EMPTY PLATE, SIR.
MENU
-Tayler-

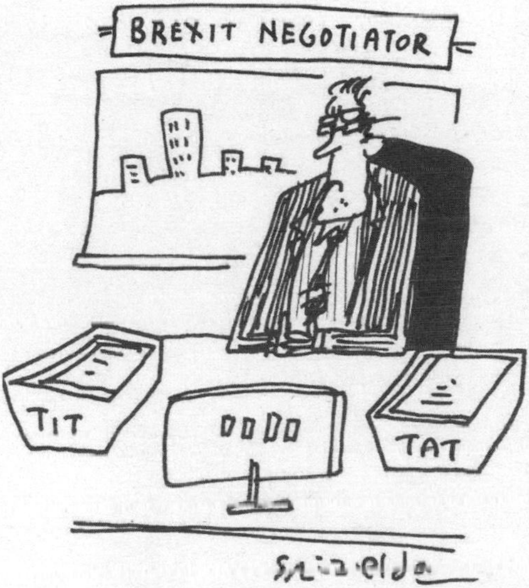
BREXIT NEGOTIATOR
TIT
TAT

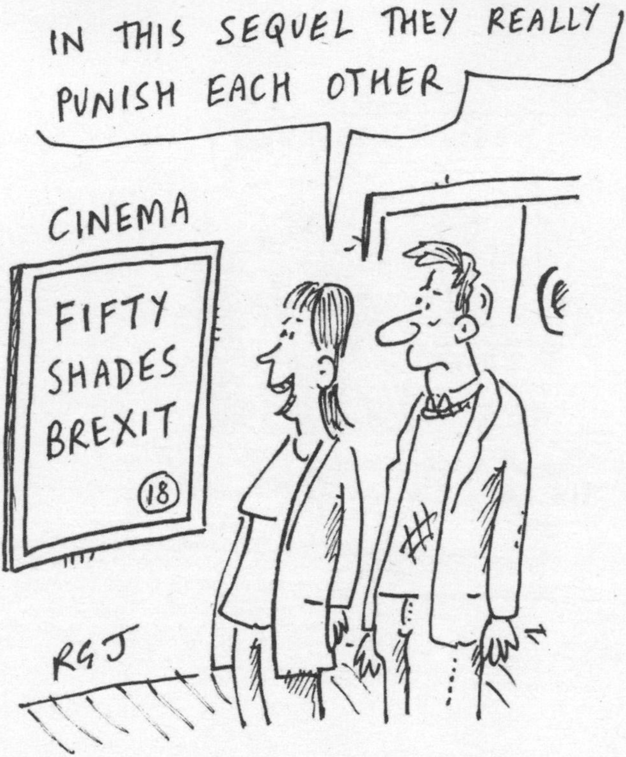
IN THIS SEQUEL THEY REALLY PUNISH EACH OTHER
CINEMA
FIFTY SHADES BREXIT
18
RGJ

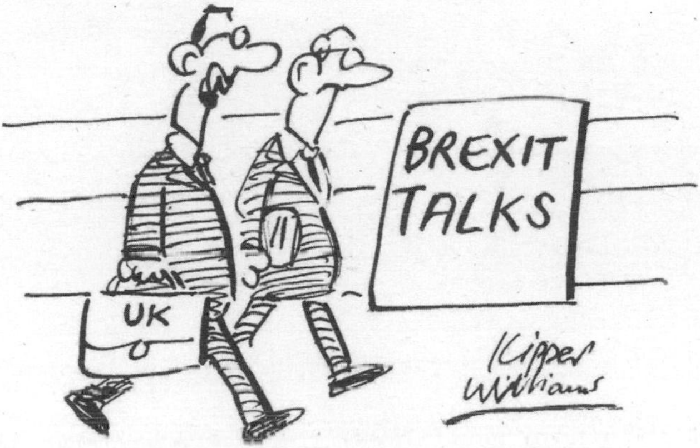
BREXIT
TALKS
UK
Kipper
Williams

‘We need a transition period so we can go from bad to worse!’

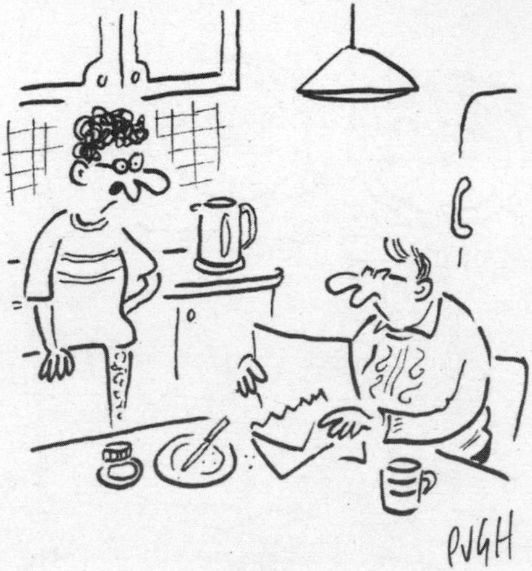
PUGH

"NO, DAD, THAT'S NOT THE BREXIT DIVORCE BILL. THAT'S MY STUDENT DEBT"

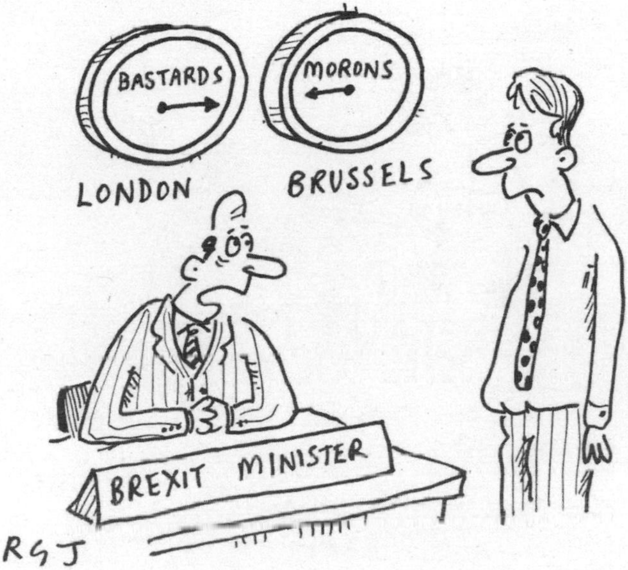
BASTARDS
MORONS
LONDON
BRUSSELS
BREXIT MINISTER
RGJ

"THE TALKS ARE NOT GOING WELL"

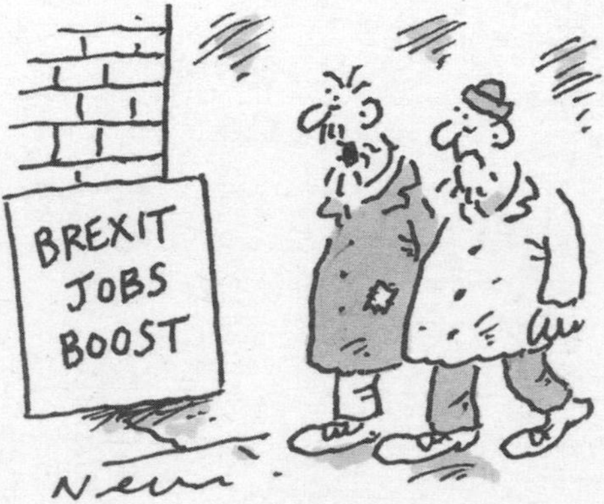
BREXIT
JOBS
BOOST

"Unfortunately, George Osborne's got them all!"

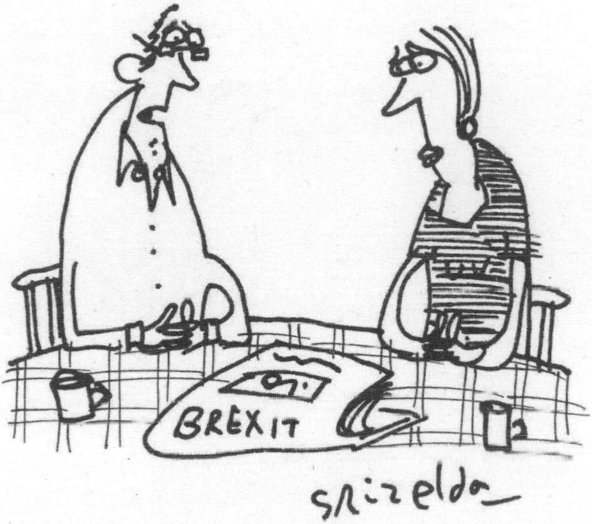
BREXIT
Grizelda

'What will we do if it's not a disaster?'

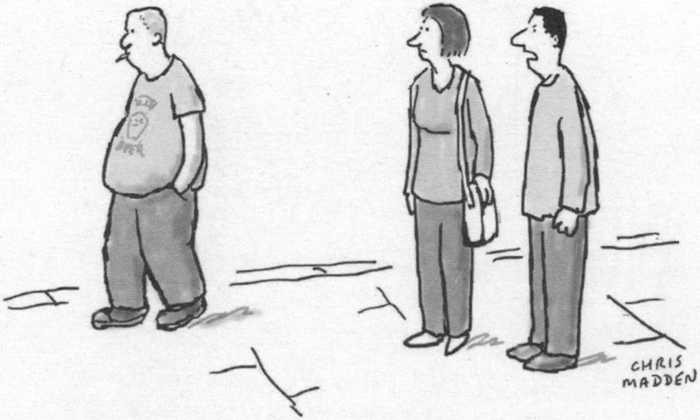
CHRIS
MADDEN

'Look – an uneducated white working class male. The sort of idiotic Brexit-voting bigot who's full of intolerance and prejudice.'

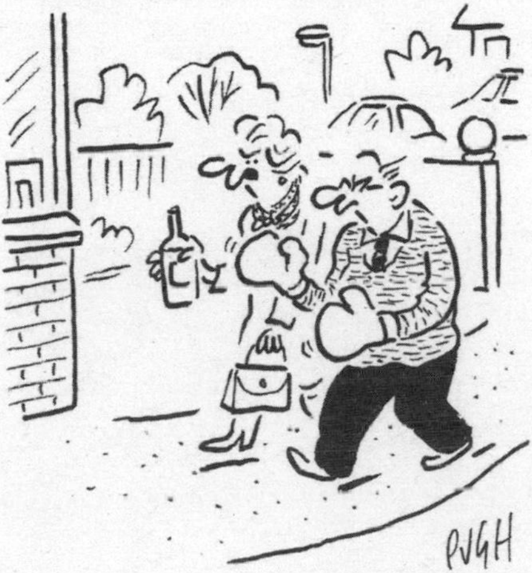
PUGH

" I KNOW YOU. YOU'RE JUST ITCHING FOR SOMEONE TO MENTION BREXIT THIS EVENING "

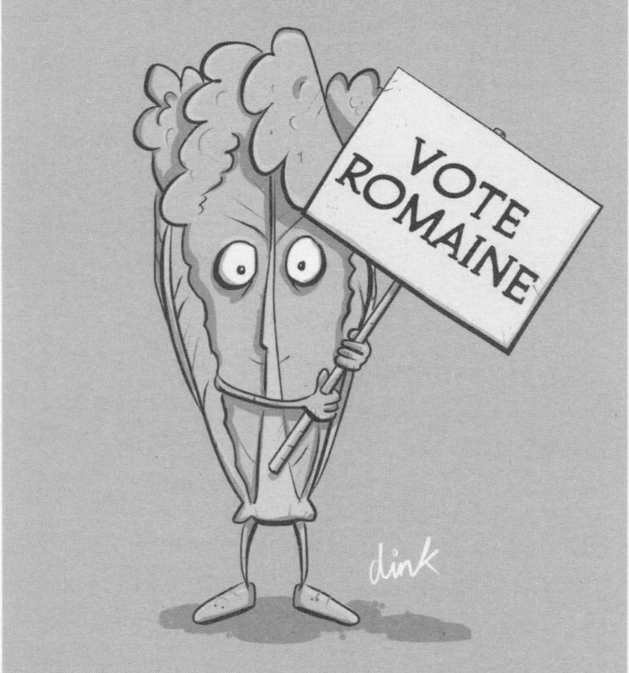
VOTE
ROMAINE
dink

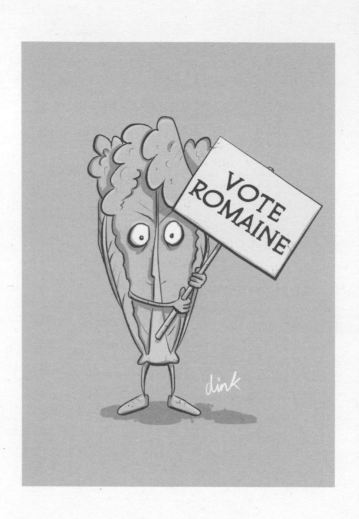

THIS IS THE MOST EXPENSIVE COLOUR EVER CREATED. IT'S CALLED "BRITISH PASSPORT BLUE"
PAINTS
£40 BILLION LEAVING FEE
RGJ

THIS PARTY IS SO DULL
I THINK I'M GOING TO
TRIGGER ARTICLE 50!

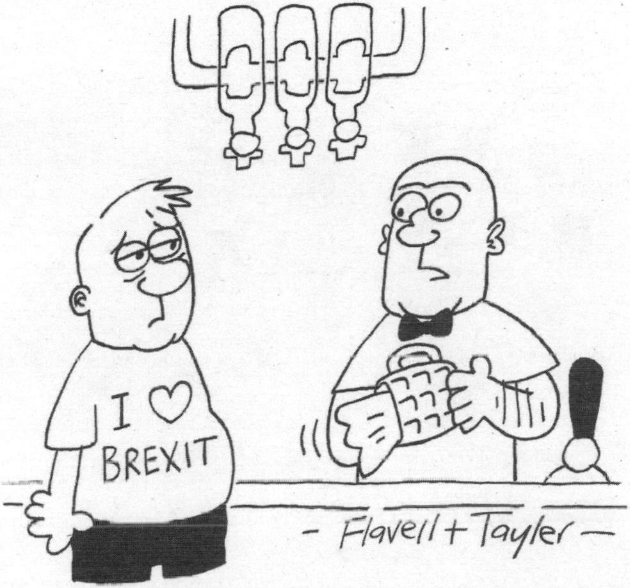
I ♡ BREXIT
- Flavell + Tayler -

"WHY THE LONG FARCE?"

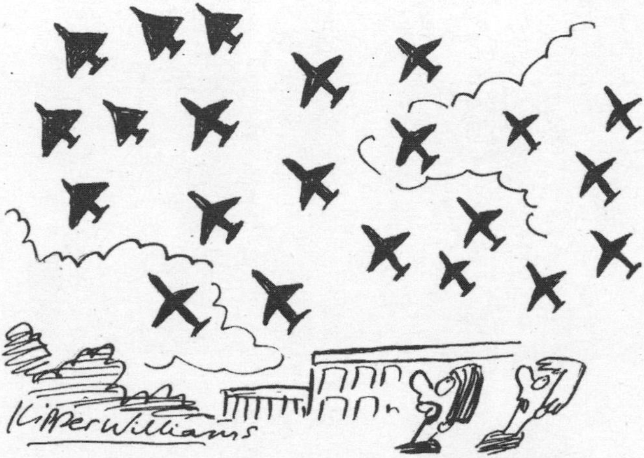
KipperWilliams

‘It’s to celebrate 100 years of Brexit negotiations!’

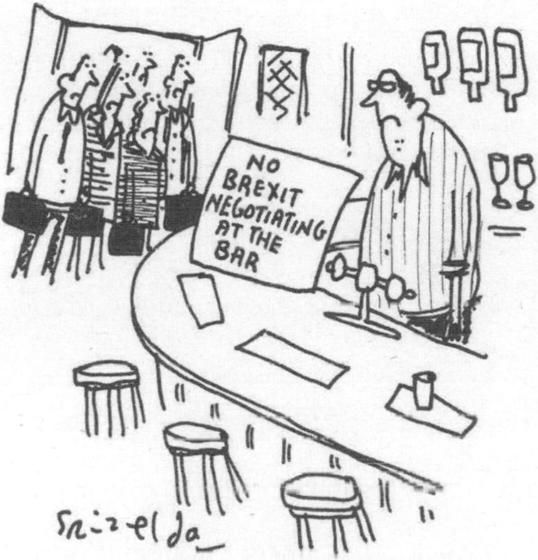
NO BREXIT NEGOTIATING AT THE BAR

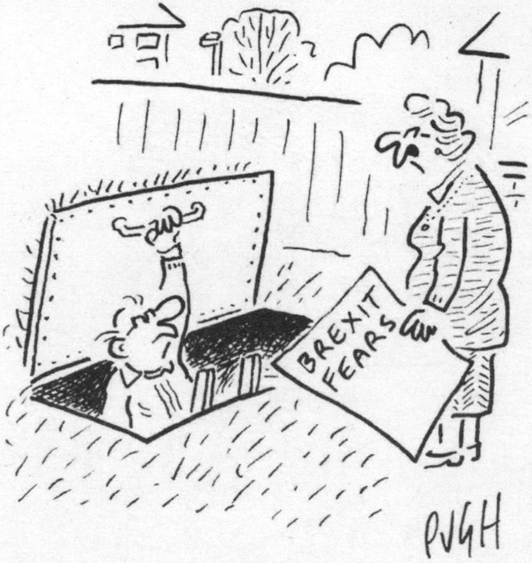
BREXIT FEARS
PUGH

"ARE YOU SURE THE BUNKER'S NECESSARY?"

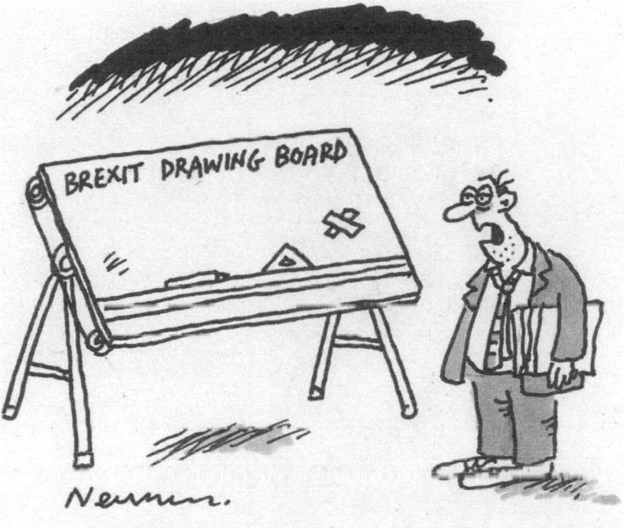
BREXIT DRAWING BOARD
Newman.

"Hello again."

Transitional
Period
Grizelda

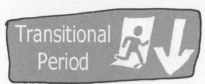

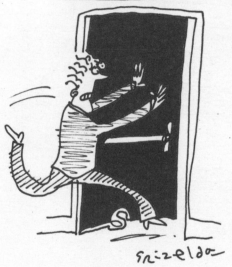

I CAN'T BELIEVE THESE TALKS ARE STILL GOING ON
BREXIT TALKS STILL STUCK
ROBO PAL 3000
HOLO-TV
RGJ

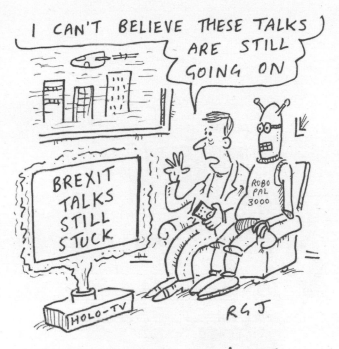

'BLADE RUNNER 2049' HAS SOME CHILLING PREDICTIONS FOR THE FUTURE

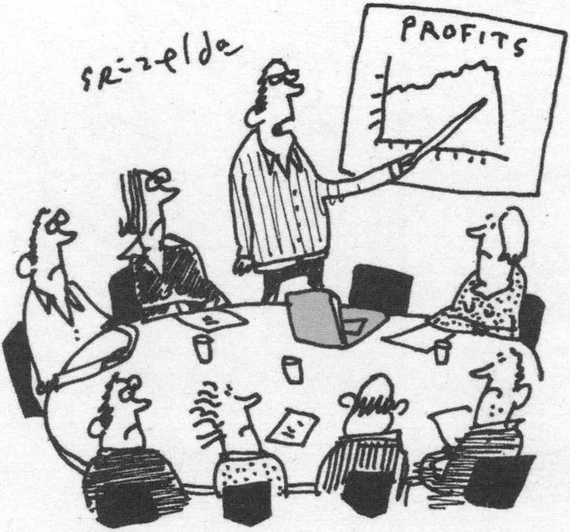
PROFITS

'I thought maybe we could
blame Brexit for this bit . . .'

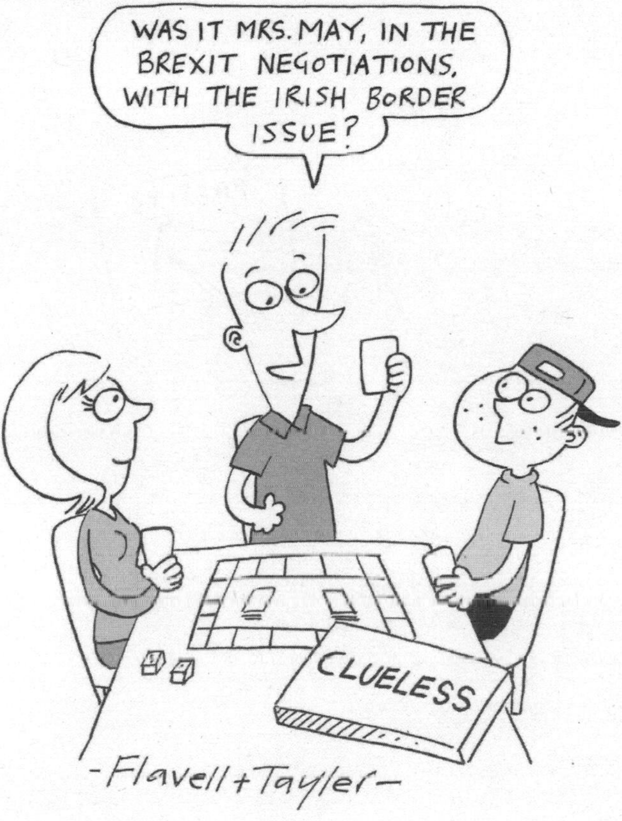
WAS IT MRS. MAY, IN THE BREXIT NEGOTIATIONS, WITH THE IRISH BORDER ISSUE?
CLUELESS
-Flavell+Tayler-

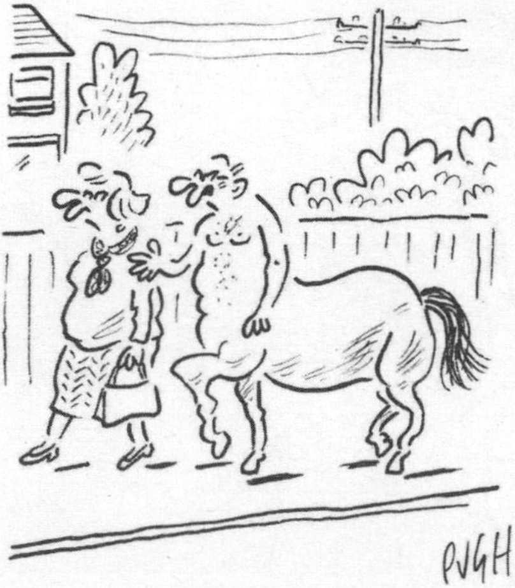
PUGH

"IT SEEMS THE WHOLE PROJECT FEAR THING WAS A COMPLETE MYTH AFTER ALL"

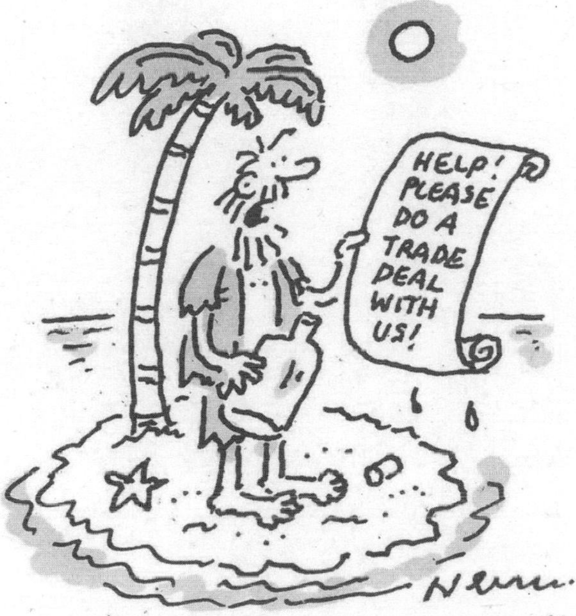
HELP! PLEASE DO A TRADE DEAL WITH US!

"It's from Liam Fox."

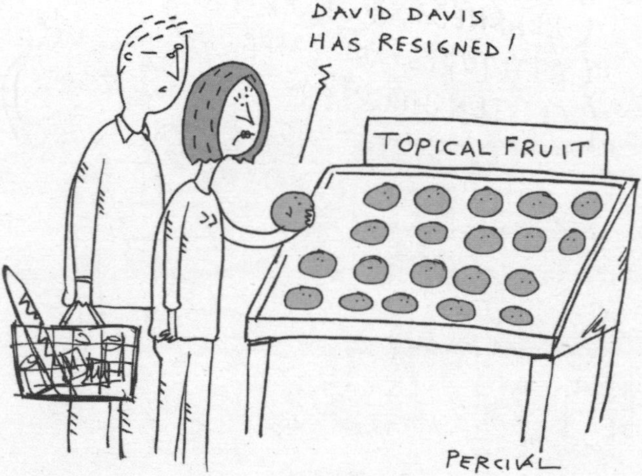
DAVID DAVIS
HAS RESIGNED!
TOPICAL FRUIT
PERCIVAL

‘They have a very short shelf life.’

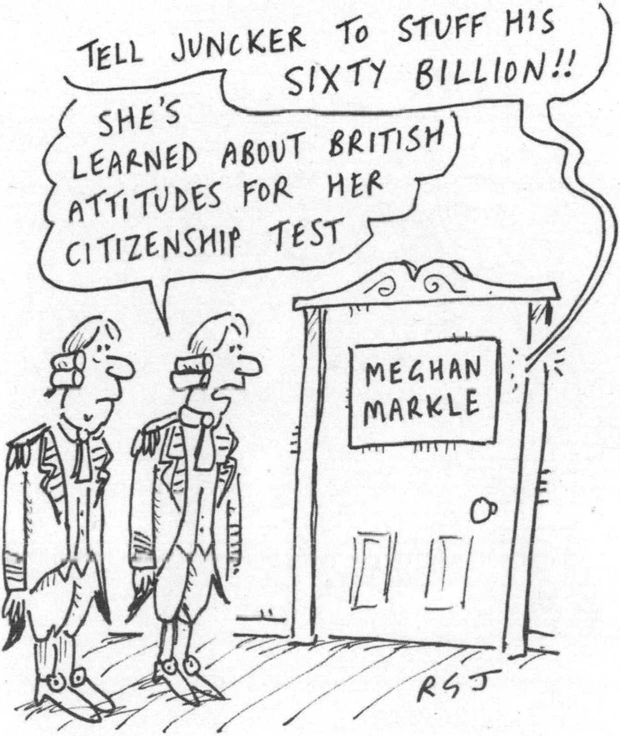

TELL JUNCKER TO STUFF HIS SIXTY BILLION!!
SHE'S LEARNED ABOUT BRITISH ATTITUDES FOR HER CITIZENSHIP TEST
MEGHAN MARKLE
RGJ

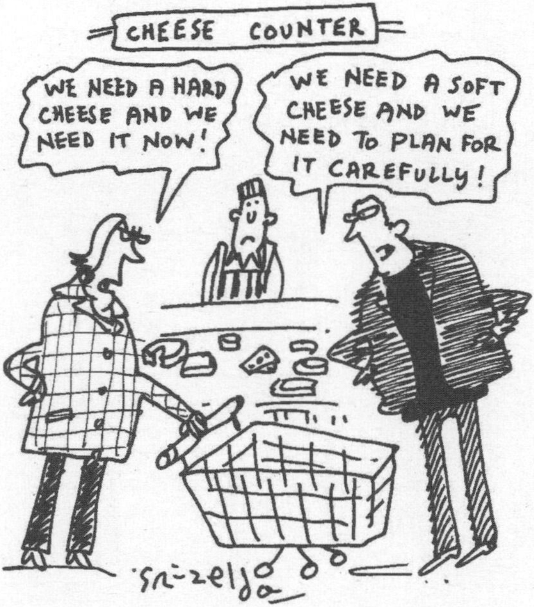
CHEESE COUNTER
WE NEED A HARD CHEESE AND WE NEED IT NOW!
WE NEED A SOFT CHEESE AND WE NEED TO PLAN FOR IT CAREFULLY!

'You drink like an EU
President!'

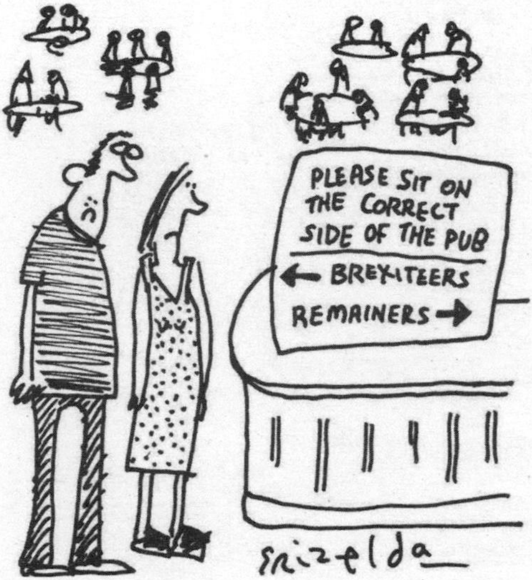
PLEASE SIT ON THE CORRECT SIDE OF THE PUB
← BREXITEERS
REMAINERS →
Grizelda

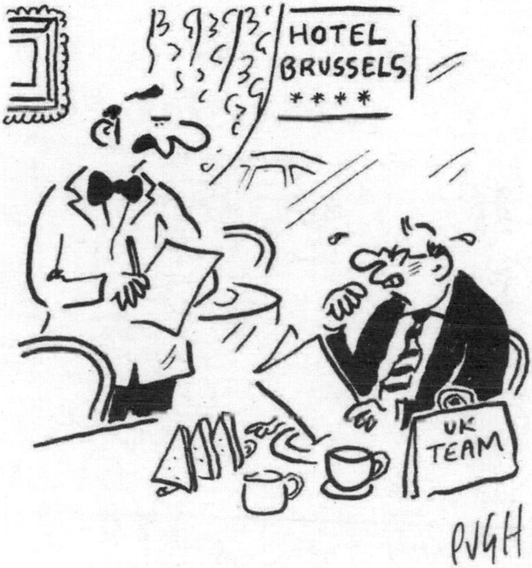
HOTEL
BRUSSELS
UK
TEAM
PUGH

"HAVE YOU DECIDED YET IF YOU WANT YOUR EGG HARD OR SOFT?"

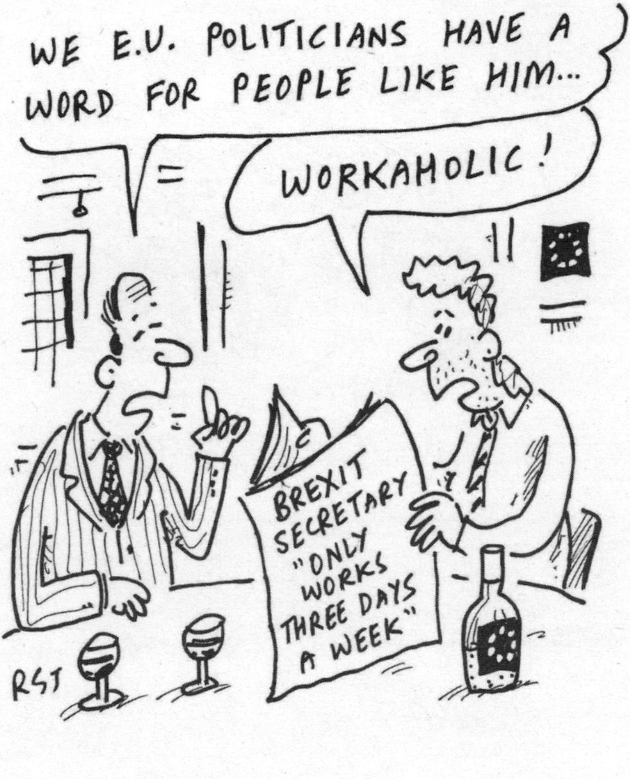
WE E.U. POLITICIANS HAVE A WORD FOR PEOPLE LIKE HIM...
WORKAHOLIC!
BREXIT SECRETARY "ONLY WORKS THREE DAYS A WEEK"
RST

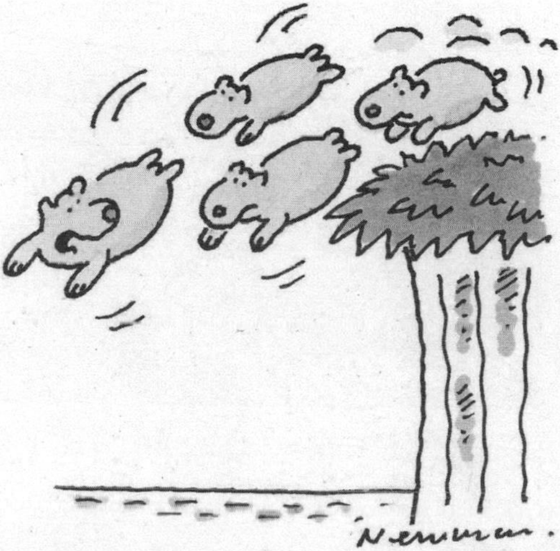
Newman.

"The deal is, we go over the cliff edge and hope for the best."

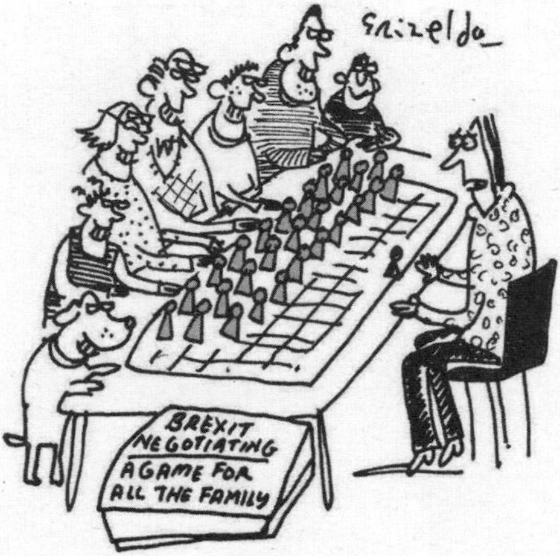
Grizelda
BREXIT NEGOTIATING
A GAME FOR ALL THE FAMILY

‘Why do *I* always have to be the UK . . . ?’

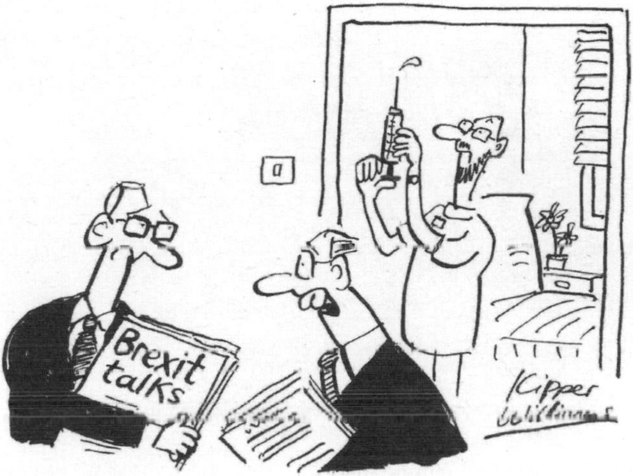
Brexit talks
Kipper

'There's always the Swiss option.'

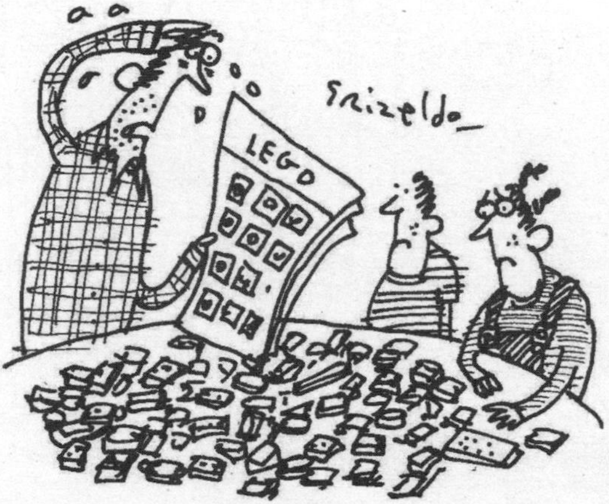
LEGO
Grizelda

'I'm sorry kids! I don't know how to build a meaningful Brexit!'

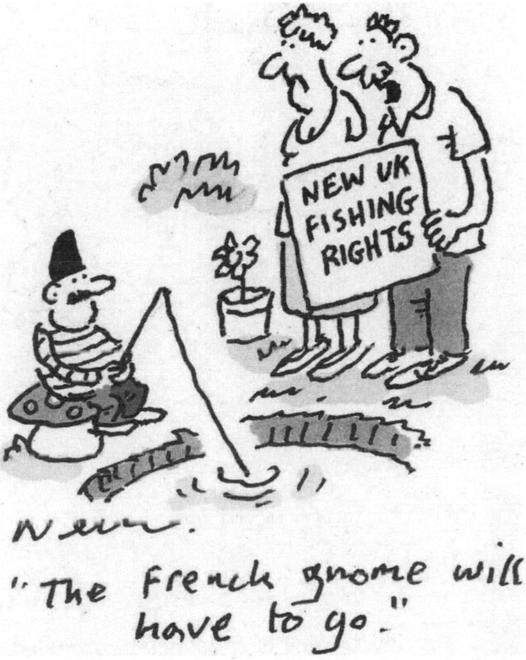
NEW UK FISHING RIGHTS
"The French gnome will have to go."

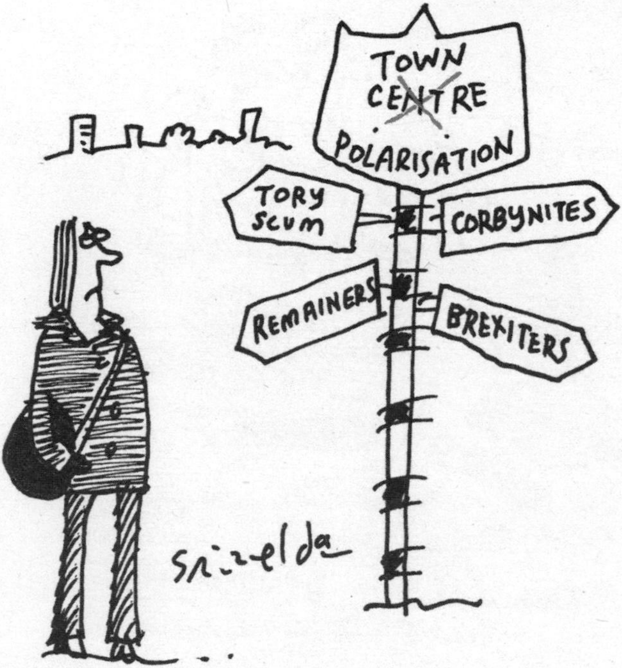
TOWN
CENTRE
POLARISATION
TORY SCUM
CORBYNITES
REMAINERS
BREXITERS
Smizzelda

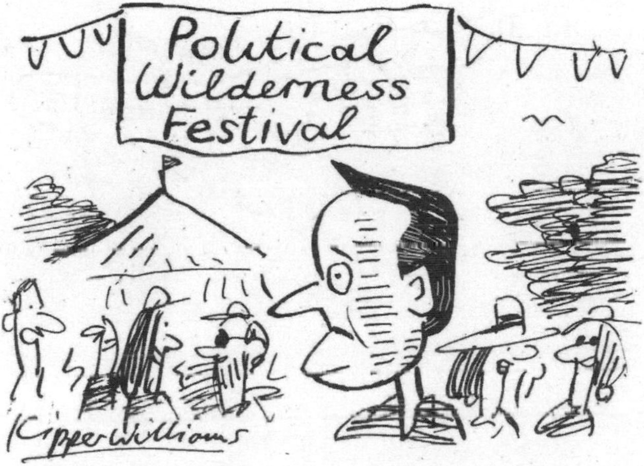
Political Wilderness Festival
Kipper Williams

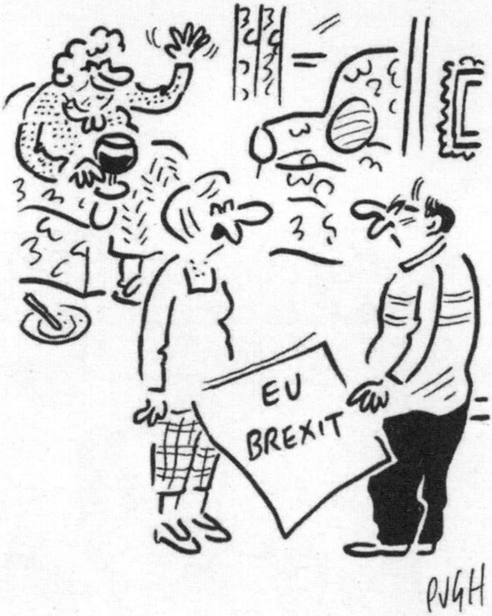
EU
BREXIT
PUGH

"WE HAVE LIFT OFF! MY MOTHER HAS SET HER DEPARTURE DATE FOR MARCH"

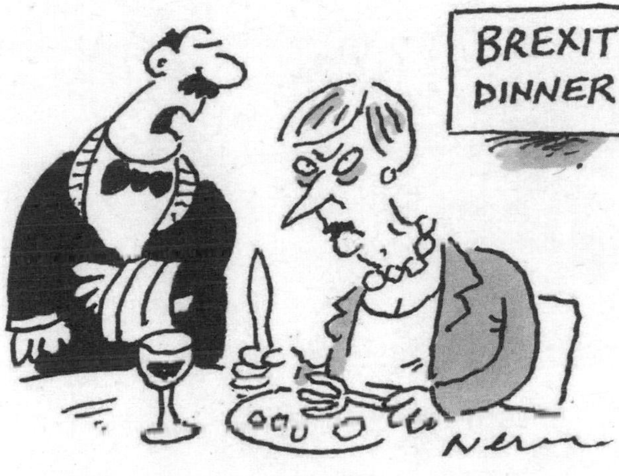
BREXIT
DINNER

'If you don't pay the bill,
you'll have to do the washing
up for 60 billion years.'

'Oh no! Hard boarders!'

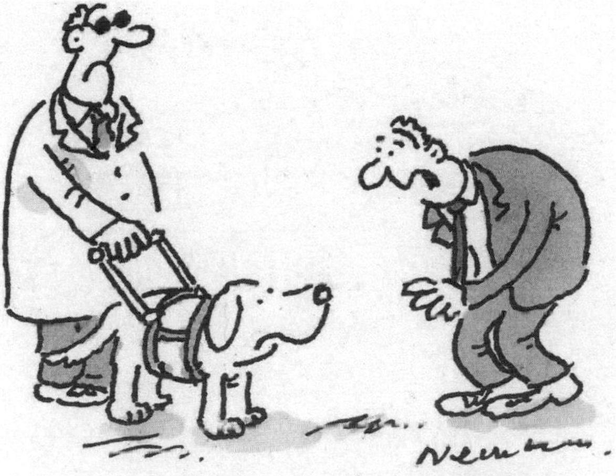
Newman.

"We need you to lead the Brexit negotiations."

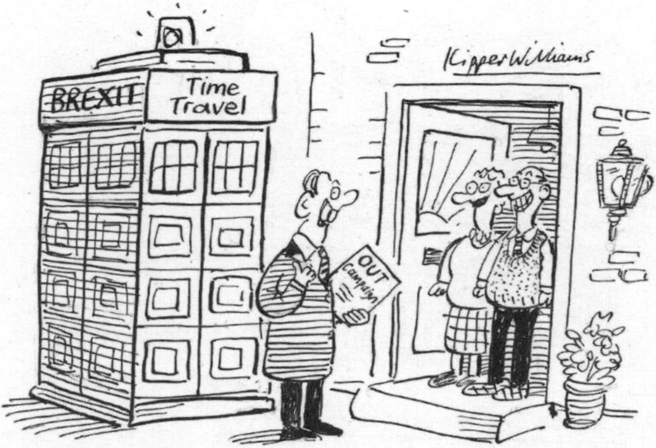
BREXIT
Time Travel
OUT Campaign
Kipper Williams

'It'll whisk you back to the sepia-tinted 1950s.'

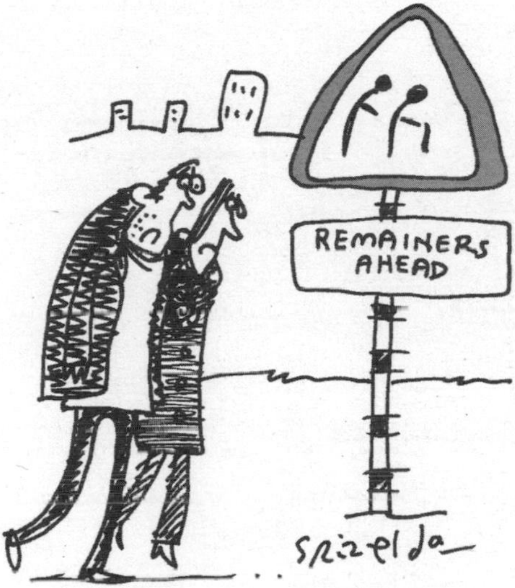
REMAINERS AHEAD
Grizelda

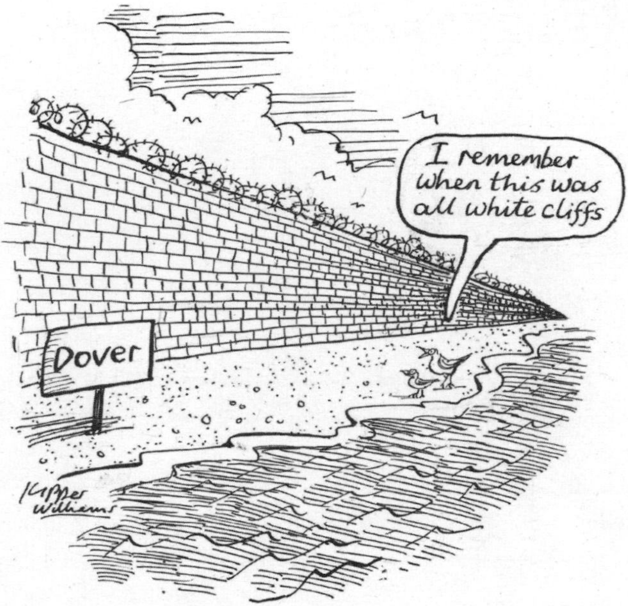
I remember when this was all white cliffs
Dover
Kipper Williams

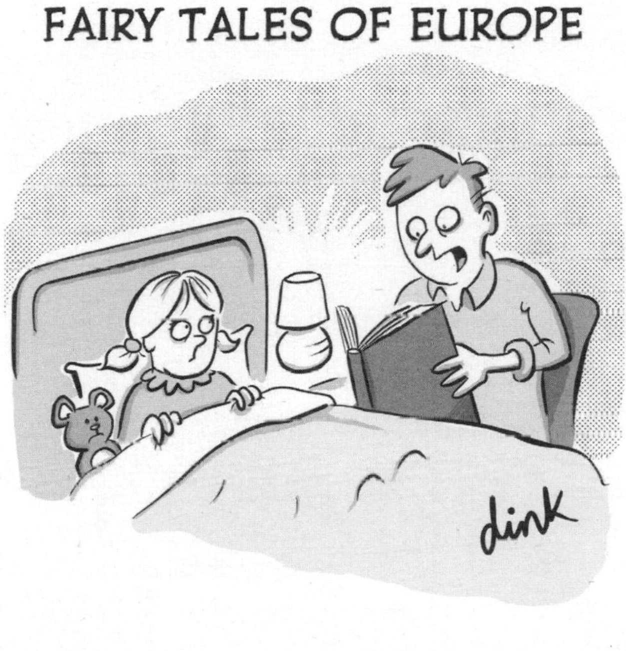
FAIRY TALES OF EUROPE
dink

'"But this Brexit is too soft," she said.'
'"And this Brexit is too hard.
But this Brexit is juuuuust . . ."'

'It's not you, it's Brexit.'

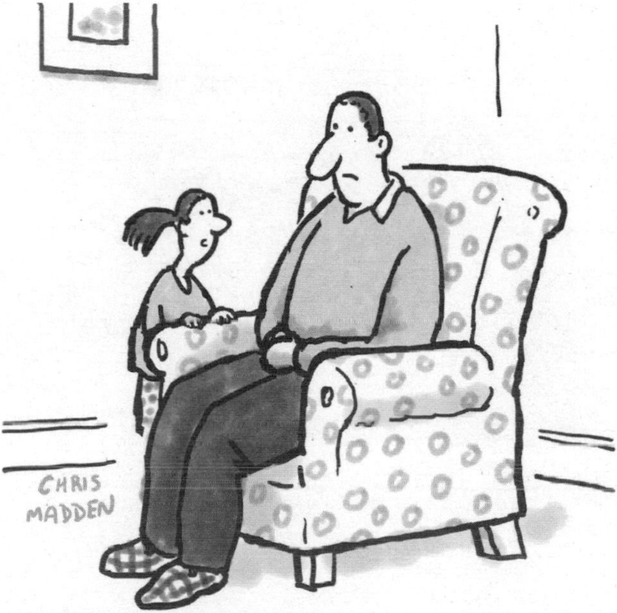
CHRIS
MADDEN

'Which way did you vote in
the Brexit Referendum, Daddy?'

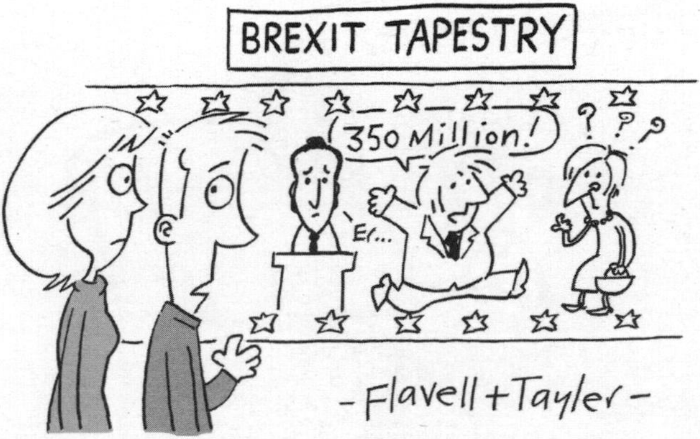
BREXIT TAPESTRY
350 Million!
Er...
? ? ?
-Flavell+Tayler-

"IT GOES ON FOR AGES, IS HARD TO UNDERSTAND AND THE BRITS LOSE..."

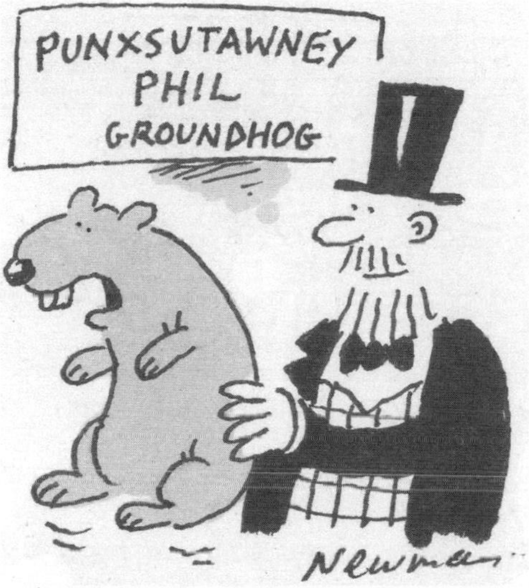
PUNXSUTAWNEY
PHIL
GROUNDHOG
Newman

'Every time I wake up it's
Brexit Day!'

'HOW MUCH DO YOU THINK WE'D
HAVE TO PAY IF WE ASKED
TO LEAVE?'

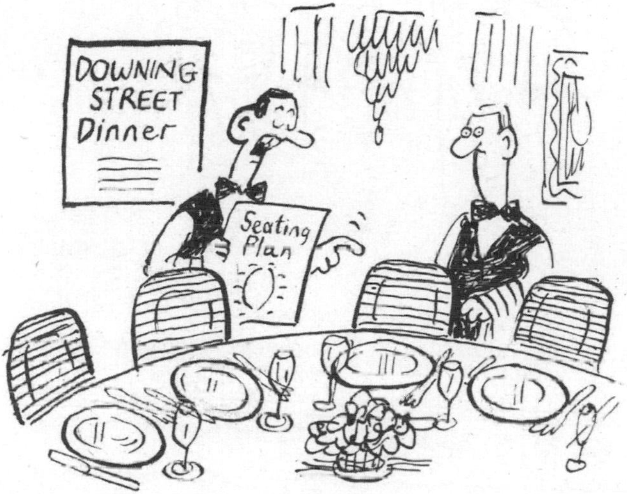
DOWNING
STREET
Dinner
Seating
Plan

'So it's hard Brexit, soft Brexit,
hard Brexit, soft Brexit . . .'

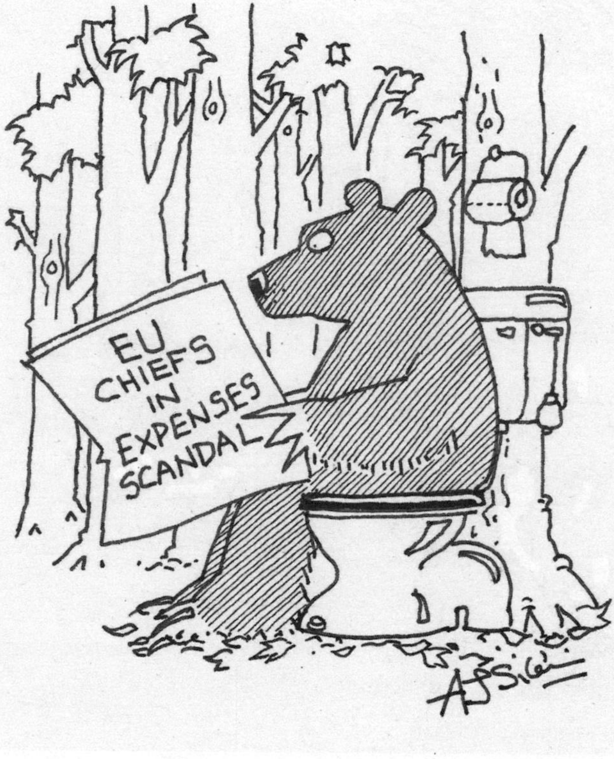
EU
CHIEFS
IN
EXPENSES
SCANDAL
AJ Singleton

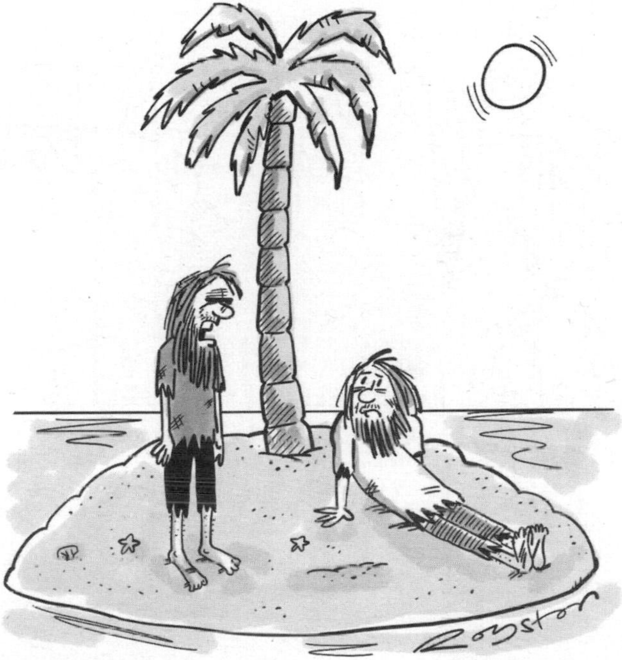
Royston

'I've decided you can stay
after the transition period.'

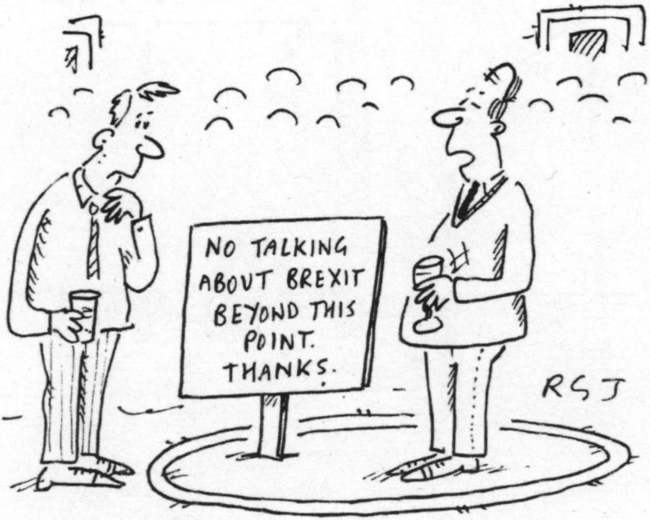
NO TALKING ABOUT BREXIT BEYOND THIS POINT. THANKS.
RGJ

'I've decided to take back control . . .'

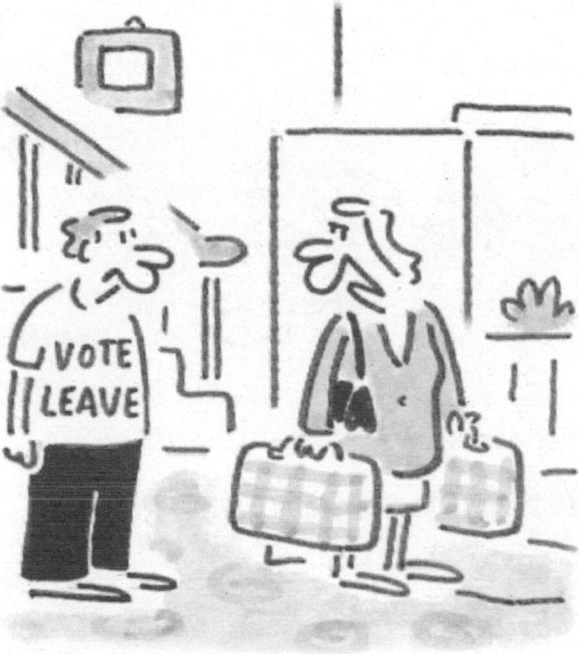
VOTE
LEAVE

'I'm leaving you for someone on a rival leave Europe campaign!'

K.J.Lamb

POST-TOOTH FAIRY

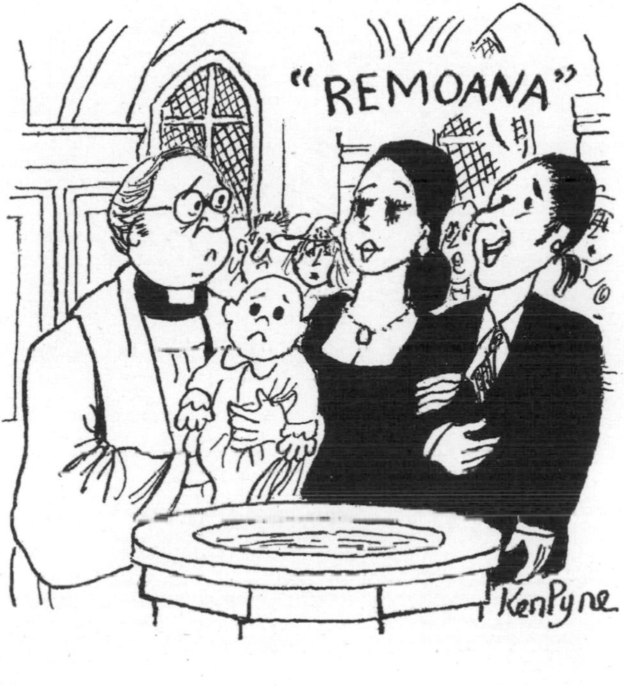
"REMOANA"
KenPyne

'I'm an EU genie. I grant
you wishes that may be
watered down or vetoed.'

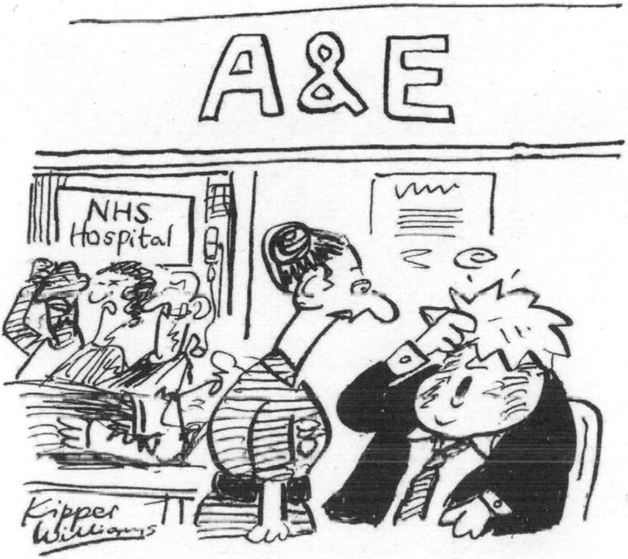
A&E
NHS
Hospital
Kipper
Williams

‘I was slapped down by
Theresa May.’

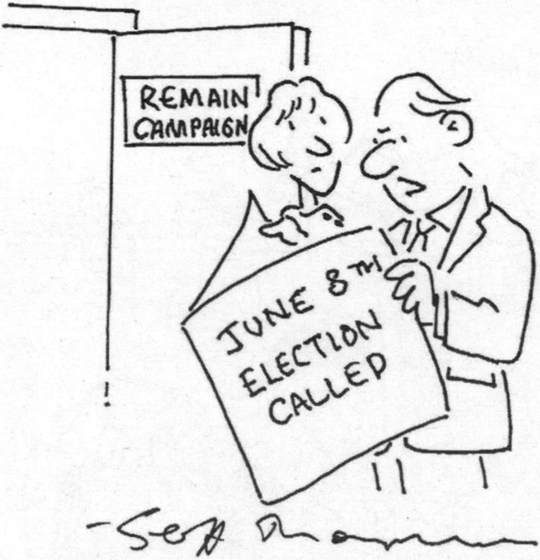
REMAIN CAMPAIGN
JUNE 8TH ELECTION CALLED

"IF WE DON'T AGREE WITH THE RESULT CAN WE HAVE ANOTHER ELECTION"

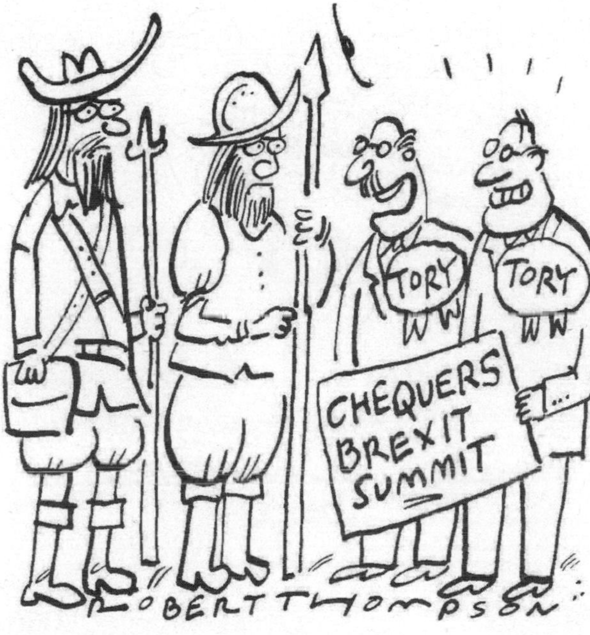
TORY
TORY
CHEQUERS BREXIT SUMMIT
ROBERT THOMPSON

‘What a coincidence! At
weekends wc drcss as Conservatives
and re-enact the Civil War too!’

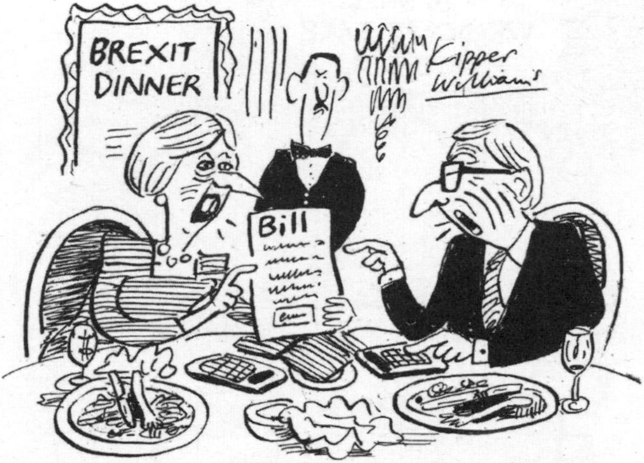
BREXIT DINNER
Bill
Kipper Williams

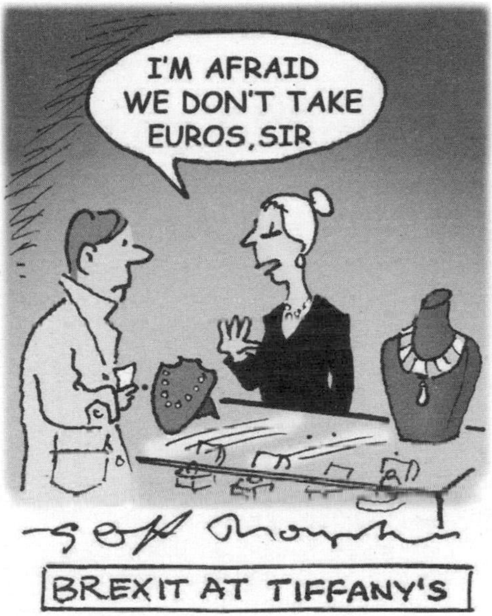
I'M AFRAID WE DON'T TAKE EUROS, SIR
BREXIT AT TIFFANY'S

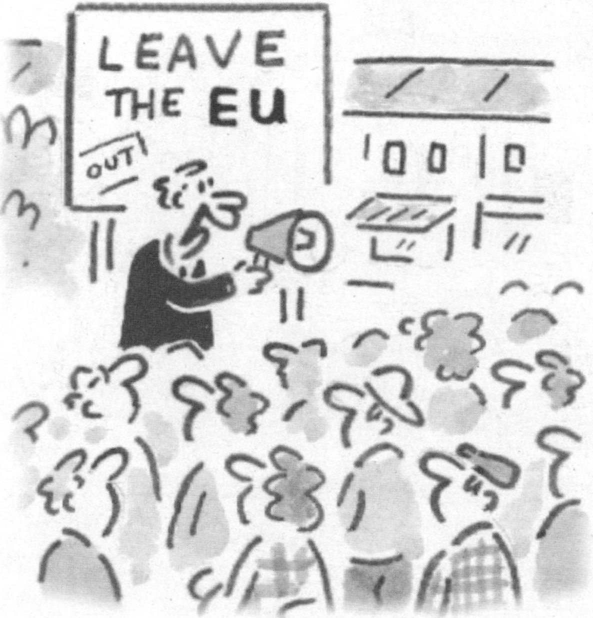
LEAVE
THE EU
OUT

'We don't need to be part of
a failing EU, we're big
enough to fail on our own!'

"IN 2017 WE ARE DETERMINED TO AVOID ANY SHOCKS TO THE E.U. SYSTEM"

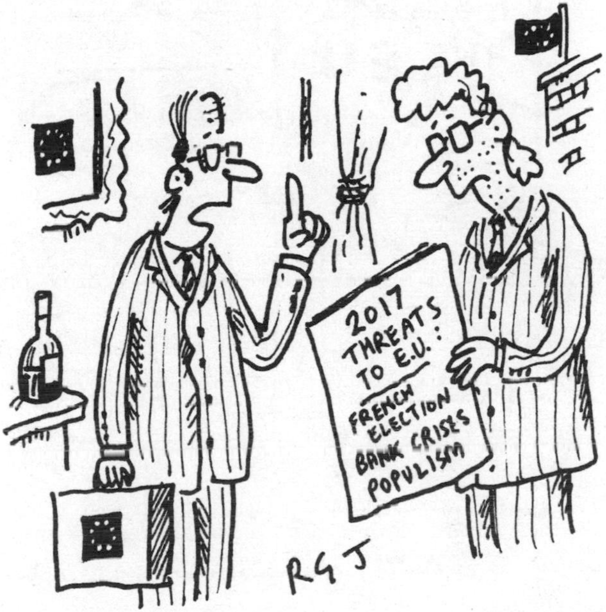
2017
THREATS TO E.U.:
FRENCH ELECTION
BANK CRISES
POPULISM
RGJ

SUCH AS REFORM

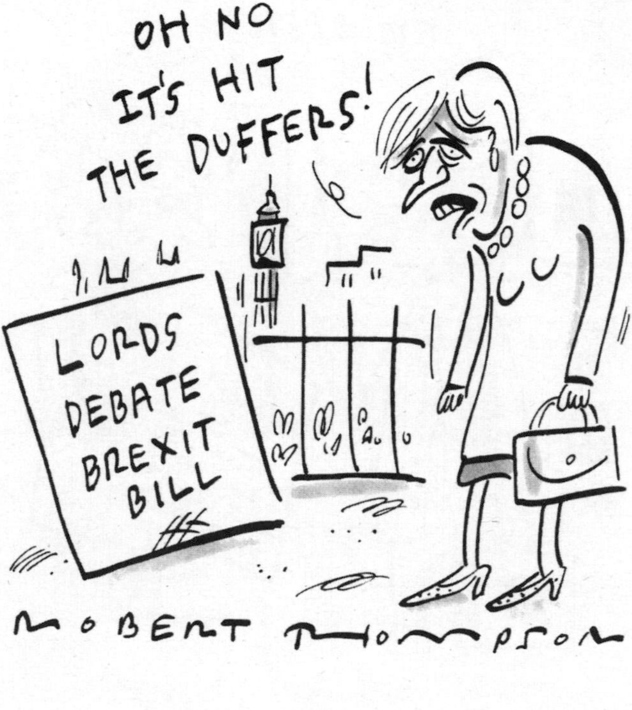
OH NO
IT'S HIT
THE DUFFERS!
LORDS
DEBATE
BREXIT
BILL
ROBERT THOMPSON

'I should have written it down. While
I was lying awake in the heat, I solved
the Irish border question.'

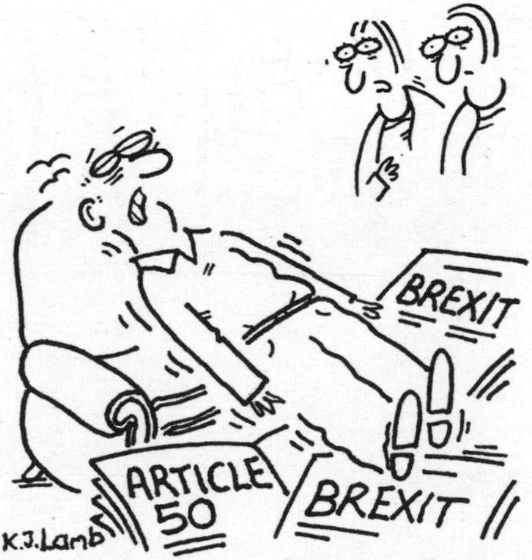
BREXIT
ARTICLE 50
BREXIT
K.J.Lamb

'OH NO – IT'S TRIGGER MORTIS'

'This Brexit is too hard and
this one is too soft . . .'

I'M GOING OUTSIDE...
IT'LL BE THE MAKING OF ME
HARD BREXIT
ROBERT THOMPSON

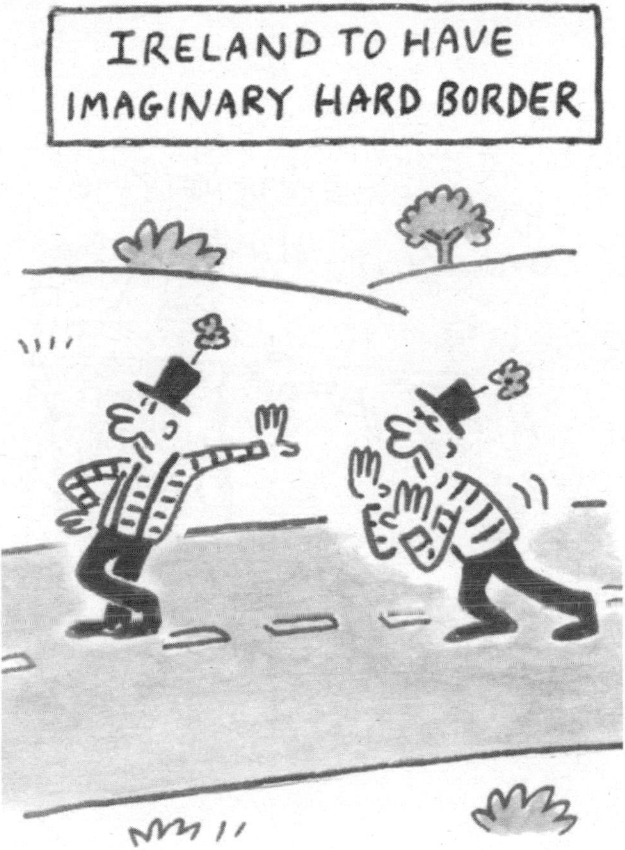
IRELAND TO HAVE IMAGINARY HARD BORDER

ARTICLE 50 TO BE TRIGGERED...
START BICKERING NOW!!
RSJ

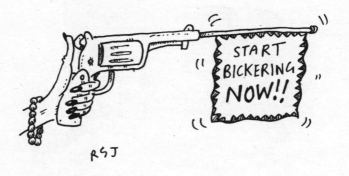

'Thank you for calling the EU.
Unfortunately nobody is available to
reject your customs plan. Your call is
not important to us.'

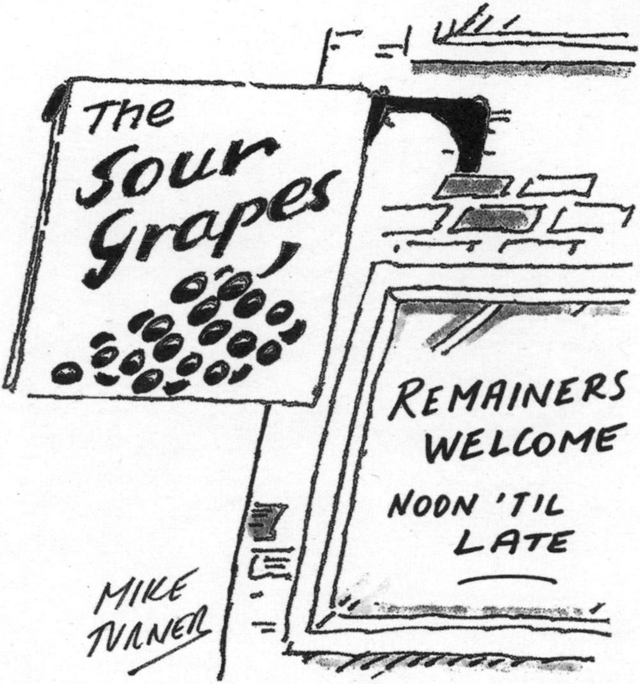
The Sour Grapes
REMAINERS WELCOME
NOON 'TIL LATE
MIKE TURNER

'Don't leave. You'll be poorer,
have less influence and it
might lead to war in Europe.'

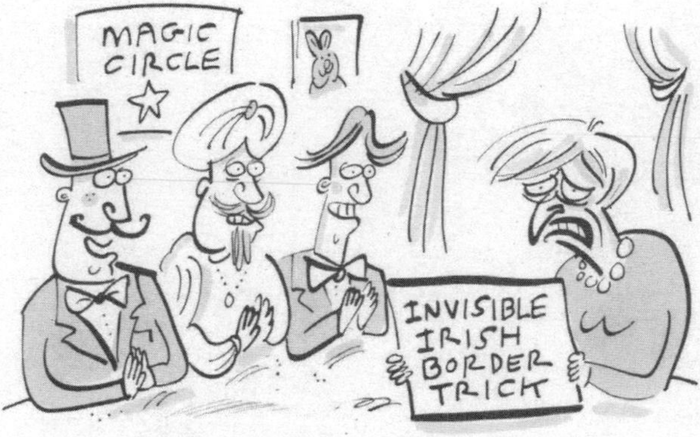

MAGIC CIRCLE
INVISIBLE IRISH BORDER TRICK

Come on Theresa your secret's safe with us ... how's it done?

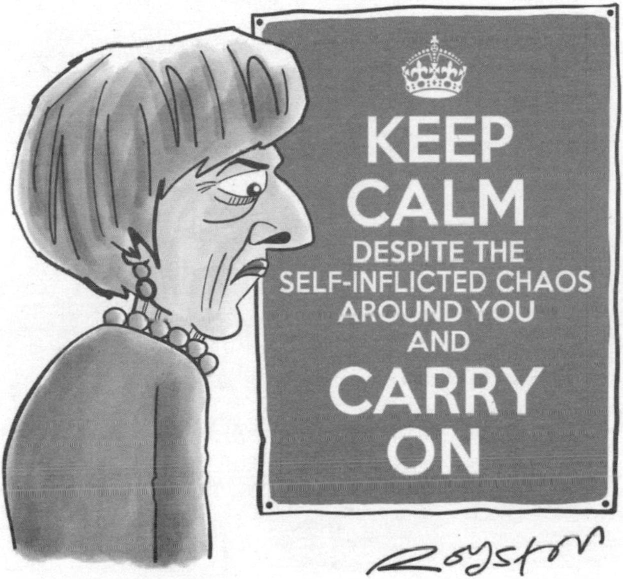
KEEP
CALM
DESPITE THE
SELF-INFLICTED CHAOS
AROUND YOU
AND
CARRY
ON
Royston

'Thank you for resigning from the shadow cabinet. Unfortunately you've called at a particularly busy time and you're being held in a queue.'

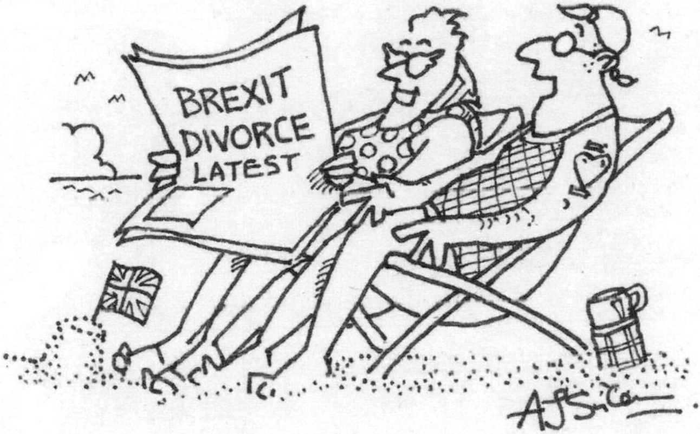
BREXIT
DIVORCE
LATEST

‘We might end up with custody of Greece.’

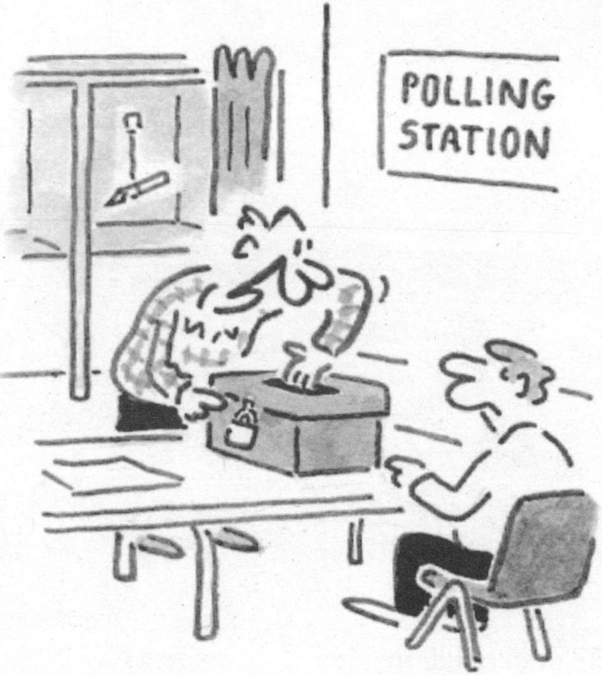
POLLING
STATION

'GET IT BACK! I've
changed my mind again!'

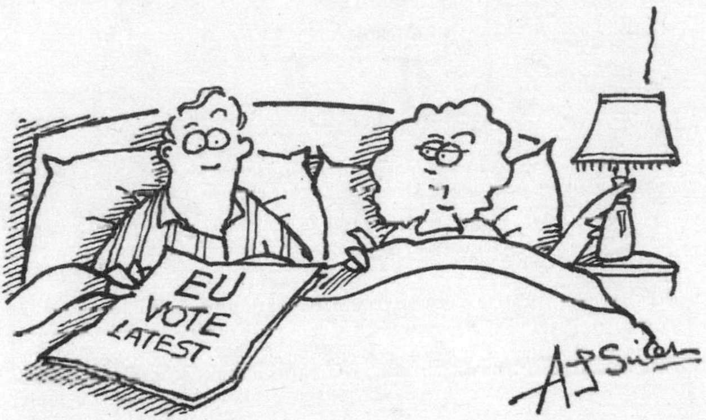
EU
VOTE
LATEST
AJSinger

'Fancy a leap in the dark?'

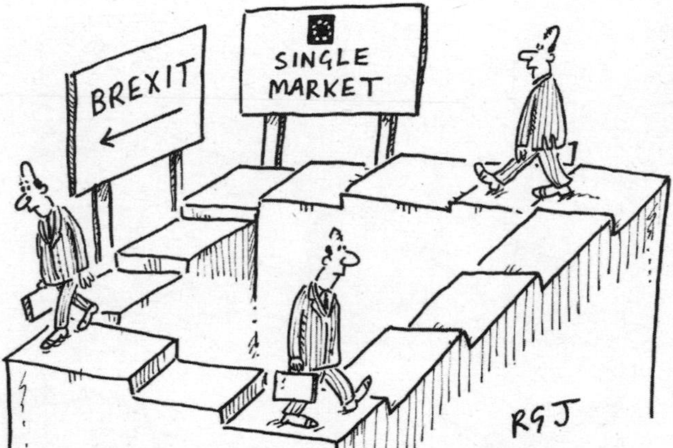
BREXIT
SINGLE
MARKET
RGJ

Those two years of Brexit
in full.

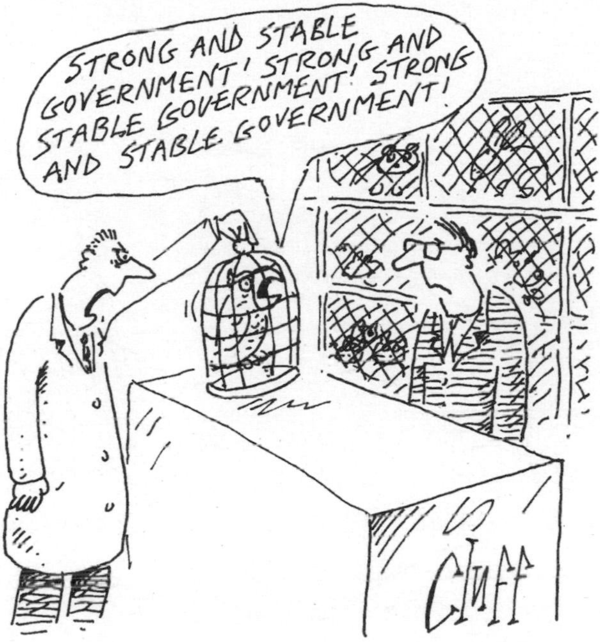
STRONG AND STABLE GOVERNMENT! STRONG AND STABLE GOVERNMENT! STRONG AND STABLE GOVERNMENT!
CLUFF

'I CAN'T GET IT TO SAY ANYTHING ELSE'

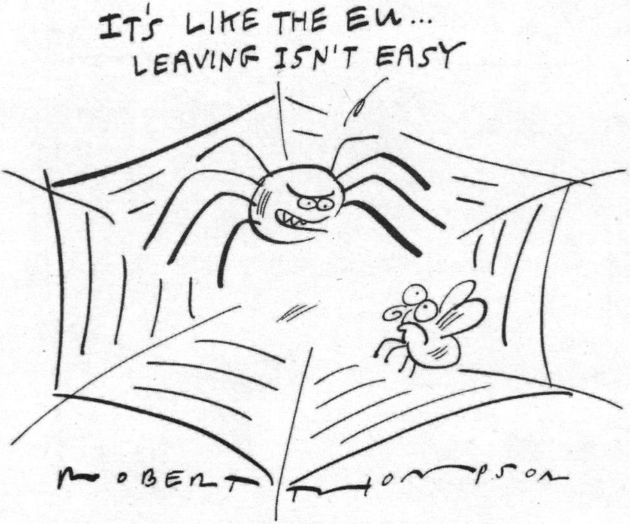
IT'S LIKE THE EU...
LEAVING ISN'T EASY
ROBERT THOMPSON

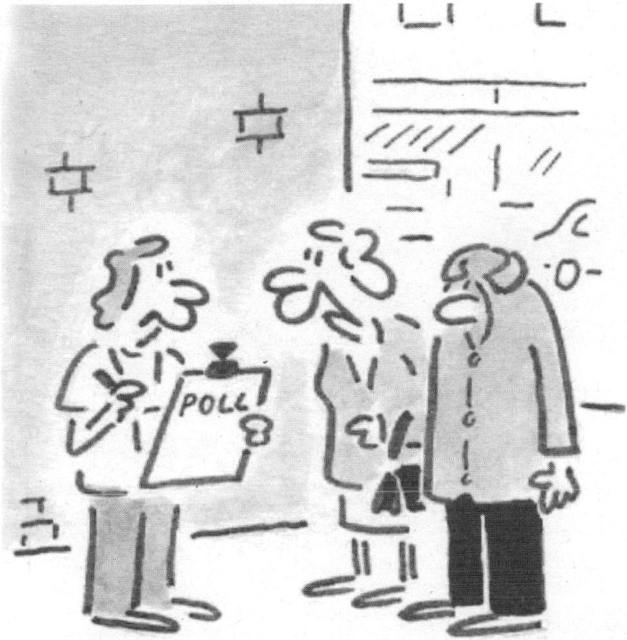
POLL

‘At the last election he was a Shy Tory, and now he’s a Bashful Leaver.’

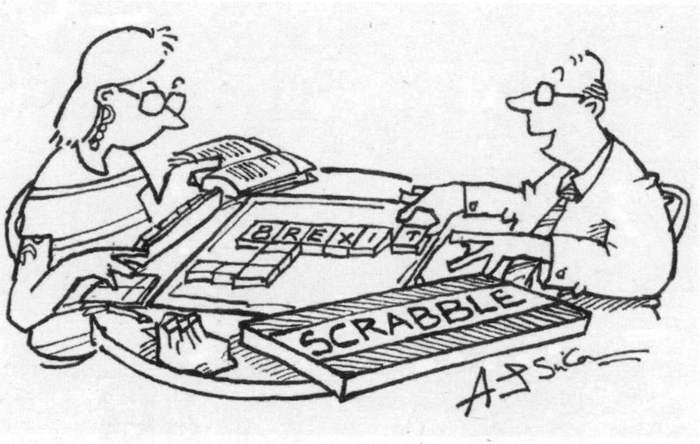
BREXIT
SCRABBLE

'Brexit. It means Brexit.'

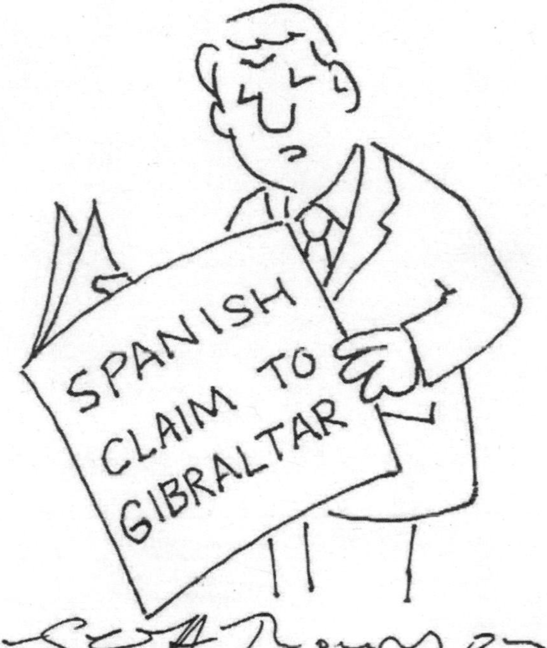
SPANISH
CLAIM TO
GIBRALTAR

'Nobody expects the
Spanish Acquisition!'

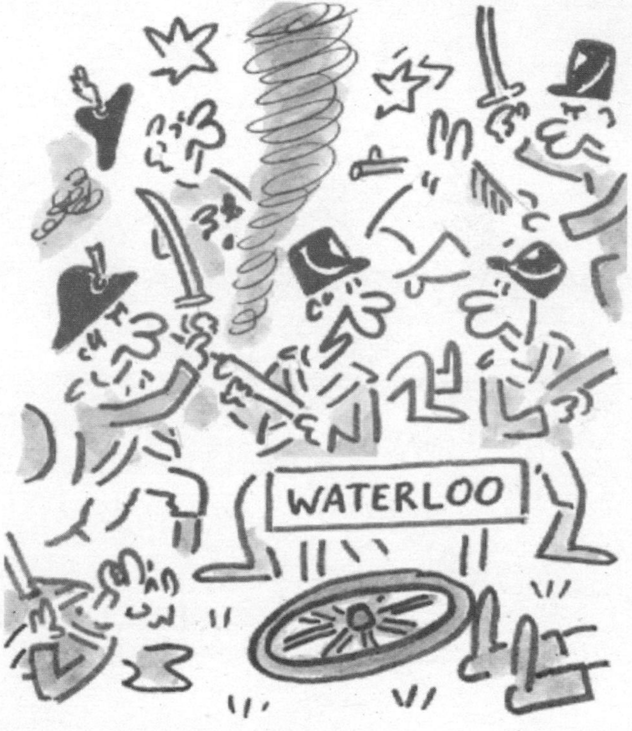
WATERLOO

'This battle has descended into a bad-tempered EU row.'

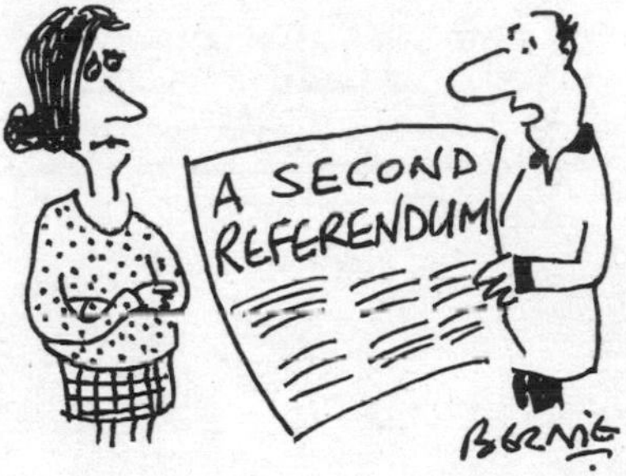
A SECOND REFERENDUM
BERNIE

"I'M FIRMLY IN THE 'OH NO' CAMP!"

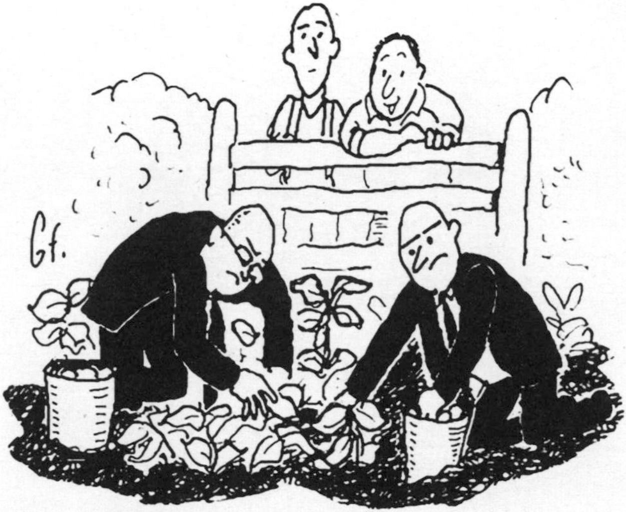
Gf.

'No Romanian fruit pickers anymore, but plenty of City bankers!'

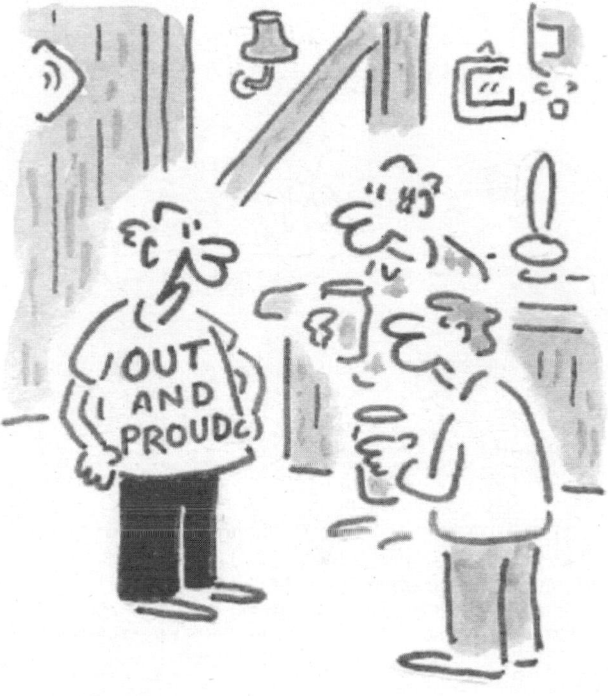
OUT
AND
PROUD

‘It’s my new *Telegraph* T-shirt.’

THOSE DISENFRANCHISED YOUNG VOTERS...

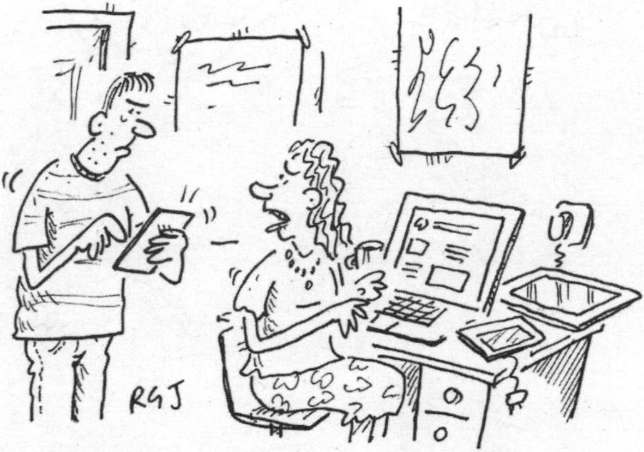
RGJ

"WE CAN'T BE IGNORED LIKE WE WERE ON BREXIT! THIS TIME LETS MAKE TEN TIMES AS MANY POSTS AND TWEETS BEFORE WE FAIL TO TURN UP TO VOTE"

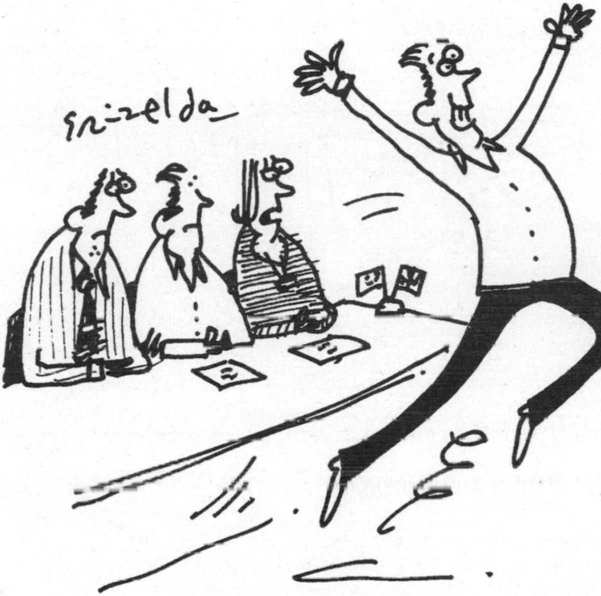
grizelda

'The EU will never accept this as a negotiating position.'

K.J.Lamb

'EXCUSE ME — I THINK YOU'LL FIND THAT THESE ARE <u>BRITISH</u> WATERS!'

'Dear John, I'm leaving you while
remaining closely aligned in
most areas. Home around 6. Mary'

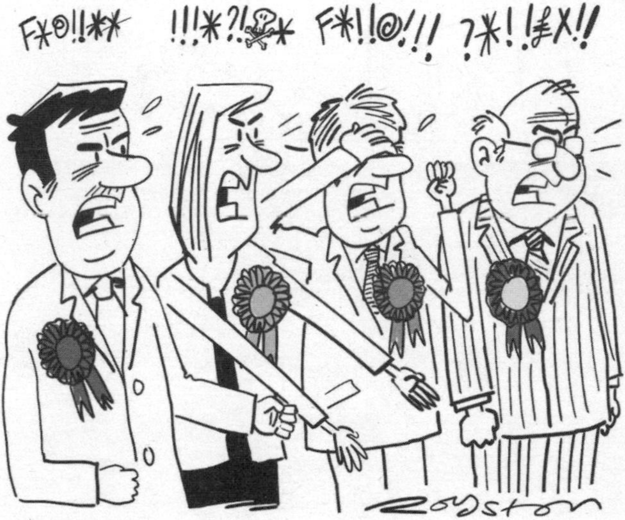
ROYSTON

Brexit: the cross party approach.

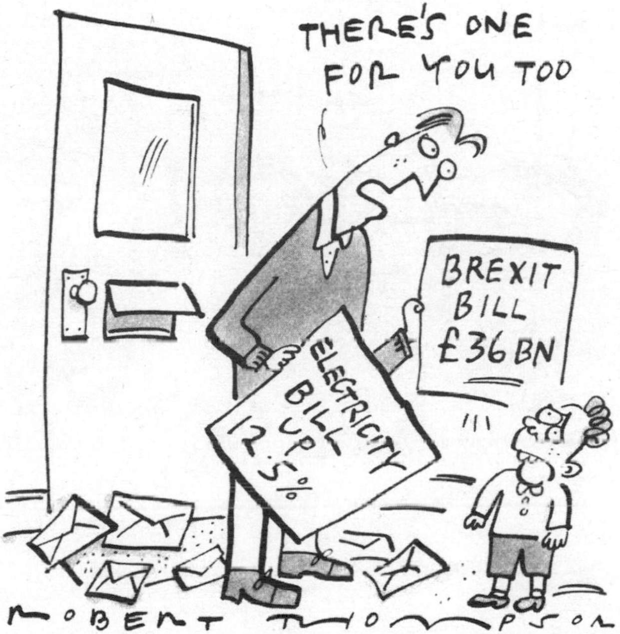
THERE'S ONE FOR YOU TOO
BREXIT BILL £36 BN
ELECTRICITY BILL UP 12.5%
ROBERT THOMPSON

'My father fought in the
Tory leadership election. He
never speaks of the things
he saw . . .'

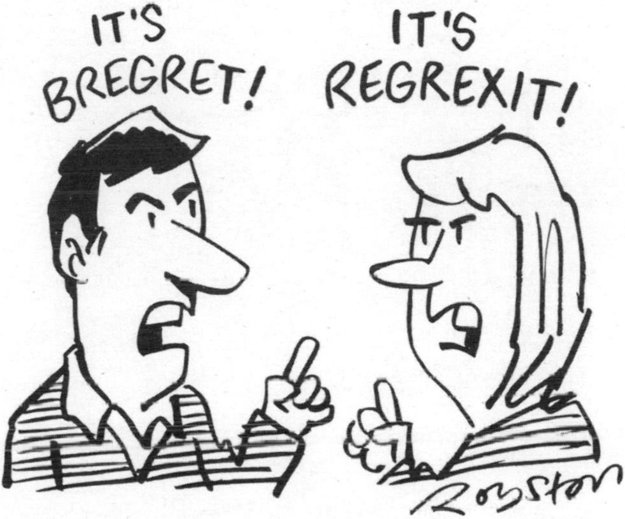
IT'S BREGRET!
IT'S REGREXIT!
Royston

A nation divided.

'We need migrants to do the jobs Brits won't or can't do. Like Prime Minister or Leader of the Opposition . . .'

1. Reproduced with kind permission of Richard Jolley (RGJ)
2. Reproduced with kind permission of Robin Flavell and Kent Tayler
3. Reproduced with kind permission of *Spectator*/ Grizelda
4. Reproduced with kind permission of Richard Jolley (RGJ)
5. Reproduced with kind permission of *Spectator*/ Kipper Williams
6. Reproduced with kind permission of the *Daily Mail*/Pugh
7. Reproduced with kind permission of Richard Jolley (RGJ)
8. Reproduced with kind permission of *Spectator*/ Nick Newman
9. Reproduced with kind permission of *Spectator*/ Grizelda
10. Reproduced with kind permission of Chris Madden
11. Reproduced with kind permission of the *Daily Mail*/Pugh
12. Reproduced with kind permission of ©dinktoons. com (Chris Williams)
13. Reproduced with kind permission of Richard Jolley (RGJ)
14. Reproduced with kind permission of *Spectator*/ Geoff Thompson
15. Reproduced with kind permission of The *New European*/Robin Flavell and Kent Tayler
16. Reproduced with kind permission of *Spectator*/ Kipper Williams
17. Reproduced with kind permission of *New Statesman*/Grizelda
18. Reproduced with kind permission of the *Daily Mail*/Pugh
19. Reproduced with kind permission of *Spectator*/ Nick Newman
20. Reproduced with kind permission of *Spectator*/ Grizelda
21. Reproduced with kind permission of Richard Jolley (RGJ)
22. Reproduced with kind permission of *Spectator*/ Grizelda
23. Reproduced with kind permission of The *New European*/Robin Flavell and Kent Tayler

24. Reproduced with kind permission of the *Daily Mail*/Pugh
25. Reproduced with kind permission of *Spectator*/Nick Newman
26. Reproduced with kind permission of *Spectator*/Matt Percival
27. Reproduced with kind permission of Richard Jolley (RGJ)
28. Reproduced with kind permission of *New Statesman*/Grizelda
29. Reproduced with kind permission of *Spectator*/Nick Newman
30. Reproduced with kind permission of *Spectator*/Grizelda
31. Reproduced with kind permission of the *Daily Mail*/Pugh
32. Reproduced with kind permission of Richard Jolley (RGJ)
33. Reproduced with kind permission of *Spectator*/Nick Newman
34. Reproduced with kind permission of *Spectator*/Grizelda
35. Reproduced with kind permission of *Spectator*/Kipper Williams
36. Reproduced with kind permission of *Spectator*/Grizelda
37. Reproduced with kind permission of *Spectator*/Nick Newman
38. Reproduced with kind permission of *Spectator*/Grizelda
39. Reproduced with kind permission of *Spectator*/Kipper Williams
40. Reproduced with kind permission of the *Daily Mail*/Pugh
41. Reproduced with kind permission of *Spectator*/Nick Newman
42. Reproduced with kind permission of *Spectator*/Grizelda
43. Reproduced with kind permission of *Spectator*/Nick Newman
44. Kipper Williams/first appeared in '*In or Out? Europe in Cartoons* (Amberley Publishing, 2016)
45. Reproduced with kind permission of *New Statesman*/Grizelda
46. Kipper Williams/first appeared in '*In or Out? Europe in Cartoons* (Amberley Publishing, 2016)

47. Reproduced with kind permission of ©dinktoons.com (Chris Williams)
48. *New Statesman*/Grizelda
49. Reproduced with kind permission of Chris Madden
50. Reproduced with kind permission of The *New European*/Robin Flavell and Kent Tayler
51. Reproduced with kind permission of *Spectator*/ Nick Newman
52. Reproduced with kind permission of *Spectator*/ Geoff Thompson
53. Reproduced with kind permission of *Spectator*/ Kipper Williams
54. Reproduced with kind permission of *Spectator*/ A. J. Singleton
55. Reproduced with kind permission of Royston Robertson (roystoncartoons.com)
56. Reproduced with kind permission of Richard Jolley (RGJ)
57. Reproduced with kind permission of the *Telegraph*/ Matt
58. Reproduced with kind permission of *PRIVATE EYE* magazine / K.J. Lamb
59. Reproduced with kind permission of *PRIVATE EYE* magazine / Ken Pyne
60. Reproduced with kind permission of the *Telegraph* / Matt
61. Reproduced with kind permission of *Spectator*/ Kipper Williams
62. Reproduced with kind permission of *Spectator*/ Geoff Thompson
63. Reproduced with kind permission of *Sunday Times*/ Robert Thompson
64. Reproduced with kind permission of *Spectator*/ Kipper Williams
65. Reproduced with kind permission of *Prospect*/Geoff Thompson
66. Reproduced with kind permission of the *Telegraph* / Matt
67. Reproduced with kind permission of *PRIVATE EYE* magazine / Richard Jolley
68. Reproduced with kind permission of *PRIVATE EYE* magazine / Robert Thompson
69. Reproduced with kind permission of the *Telegraph* / Matt
70. Reproduced with kind permission of *PRIVATE EYE* magazine / K.J. Lamb

71. Reproduced with kind permission of the *Telegraph*/Matt

72. Reproduced with kind permission of *PRIVATE EYE* magazine / Robert Thompson

73. Reproduced with kind permission of the *Telegraph*/Matt

74. Reproduced with kind permission of *PRIVATE EYE* magazine / Richard Jolley

75. Reproduced with kind permission of the *Telegraph*/Matt

76. Reproduced with kind permission of *PRIVATE EYE* magazine / Mike Turner

77. Reproduced with kind permission of the *Telegraph*/Matt

78. Reproduced with kind permission of *Mail on Sunday*/Geoff Thompson

79. Reproduced with kind permission of Royston Robertson (roystoncartoons.com)

80. Reproduced with kind permission of the *Telegraph*/Matt

81. Reproduced with kind permission of *Spectator*/A. J. Singleton

82. Reproduced with kind permission of the *Telegraph*/Matt

83. Reproduced with kind permission of *Spectator*/A. J. Singleton

84. Reproduced with kind permission of *PRIVATE EYE* magazine / Richard Jolley

85. Reproduced with kind permission of *PRIVATE EYE* magazine / Cluff

86. Reproduced with kind permission of the *Spectator*/Robert Thompson

87. Reproduced with kind permission of the *Telegraph*/Matt

88. Reproduced with kind permission of *Spectator*/A. J. Singleton

89. Reproduced with kind permission of *Spectator*/Geoff Thompson

90. Reproduced with kind permission of the *Telegraph*/Matt

91. Reproduced with kind permission of *PRIVATE EYE* magazine / Bernie

92. Reproduced with kind permission of *PRIVATE EYE* magazine / Geoff Royall

93. Reproduced with kind permission of the *Telegraph* / Matt

94. Reproduced with kind permission of *PRIVATE EYE* magazine / Richard Jolley
95. Reproduced with kind permission of *PRIVATE EYE* magazine / Grizelda
96. Reproduced with kind permission of *PRIVATE EYE* magazine / K.J. Lamb
97. Reproduced with kind permission of the *Telegraph* / Matt
98. Reproduced with kind permission of Royston Robertson (roystoncartoons.com)
99. Reproduced with kind permission of *PRIVATE EYE* magazine / Robert Thompson
100. Reproduced with kind permission of the *Telegraph* / Matt
101. Reproduced with kind permission of *PRIVATE EYE* magazine / Royston Robertson (roystoncartoons.com)
102. Reproduced with kind permission of the *Telegraph* / Matt